I used to be _____

I used to be ___

HOW to NAVIGATE LARGE and SMALL LOSSES in LIFE and FIND YOUR PATH FORWARD

CHUCK and ASHLEY ELLIOTT

Revell

a division of Baker Publishing Group
Grand Rapids, Michigan

Published by Revell
a division of Baker Publishing Group
Grand Rapids, Michigan
www.revellbooks.com

Printed in the United States of America

Library of Congress Cataloging-in-Publication Data
Names: Elliott, Chuck, 1982– author. | Elliott, Ashley S., 1984– author.
Title: I used to be : how to navigate large and small losses in life and
   find your path forward / Chuck and Ashley Elliott.
Description: Grand Rapids, Michigan : Revell, a division of Baker Publishing
   Group, 2023. | Includes bibliographical references. |
Identifiers: LCCN 2022061702 | ISBN 9780800742492 (paperback) | ISBN
   9780800743147 (casebound) | ISBN 9781493441303 (ebook)
Subjects: LCSH: Grief—Religious aspects—Christianity. | Loss (Psychology)—
   Religious aspects—Christianity. | Hope—Religious aspects—Christianity.
Classification: LCC BV4905.3 .E42 2023 | DDC 248.8/6—dc23/eng/20230324

The names and details of the people and situations described in this book have been changed or presented in composite form in order to ensure the privacy of those with whom the author has worked.

Cover and interior design by William Overbeeke
Illustrations by Olivia Stallmer

23   24   25   26   27   28   29   7   6   5   4   3   2   1

To those we have lost,
we miss you.
To those who have lost,
we see you.

contents

1   who I used to be

WHEN YOU SAW THE TITLE OF THIS BOOK, process how you filled in the blank. Perhaps you were flooded with memories from the past, taken back to how it used to be. If your stomach twisted a bit as you thought of how things have changed, you're not alone. In the Bible, one of the psalmists declared, "My heart is breaking as I remember how it used to be" (Ps. 42:4). We've all changed a bit over the years. Some of these changes have been desirable, while others have been difficult to process. We, Chuck and Ashley, have gained friends. We've been offered jobs. We've lost friends, loved ones, and opportunities. Imagine the ways you've changed. During our time together, we want to help you process who you used to be in comparison with who you are now and who you would like to be in the future. We'll ask you some contemplative questions and use a fill-in-the-blank prompt to facilitate reflection and growth. And we'll share who we used to be and who we are working to become. Let's dive in.

I used to be _____. Think of that sentence. How would *you* fill in the blank? I used to be _____.

We used to be <u>expecting a child</u>. In 2015, 2016, and 2017, we faced recurrent miscarriage. We used to be other things as well. We used to be neighbors to some great friends who moved away. We used to be employed at different workplaces. We've faced times of financial insecurity, and we've grieved over changes in the church. Long before we lost our tiny children to death, we faced relational grief. I, Chuck, used to be <u>trusted</u>. Just two months before our wedding, Ashley found pornographic images on my computer. Even though I've not looked at those kinds of images since then, the relational costs still impact our marriage today. We've grieved lost co-workers, affairs, and death. And some of the positive changes in our lives have brought grief to others. Going to college, getting married, and gaining new jobs have brought changes to relationships, which stirred up strong emotions—even grief.

Consider the positive and negative things you used to be. Whatever you used to be could have resulted from your own behavior, the actions of others, or some other cause. Whatever brought the loss, there is hope. This isn't a book about miscarriage or relational failure. This book is about you. Maybe you used to be a spouse, a parent, or an employee; perhaps you had an abortion, are struggling with addiction, or moved away from family to support your spouse and would say that you used to be "happy."

This book is about you. Though we will share some personal stories from our journey, our desire is to help you process *your* loss, identify the joy that came from the past role, heal from the events that invaded your life, and discover purpose as you move forward. We will share portions of stories from friends, clients, and church members who faced divorce, job loss, or the death of a spouse. I, Chuck, will share from my expertise as a pastor, and I, Ashley, will share from my experience as a faith-based counselor and educator. We have developed concepts to help verbalize some of the encounters we and others have faced. You'll learn about unwanted titles, how to establish an exit plan, and how to escape negative spaces. You'll have more tools in your toolbox that will help you heal so you can leave a legacy. We'll provide examples of both large and small losses, and we trust that you'll be able to apply lessons from others' situations and find strength here. At the end of each chapter, we'll practice bringing God into the midst of our loss by praying together.

As we faced tragedy after tragedy in our marriage and parenting journey, we continued to get up. In time, we grew stronger and found that our stride became a little smoother. As we moved forward, we knew so many others who were still stuck. We decided to invite them to join us on the journey toward healing. But first, we needed oxygen. We pulled down the oxygen mask, took some deep breaths, and found ourselves able to breathe and think a little more clearly. Since then, we've caught our breath a bit and passed the oxygen to others, and now we're passing the oxygen mask on to you. Place the mask to your face, inhale deeply, and begin to catch your breath. Down the road, someone else will need the hope that you've found. Our prayer is that you will be ready to see them and offer some oxygen to their weary lungs.

Understanding Ourselves

We may find ourselves perplexed by our response to deep grief. At times we may be surprised at how strong we must appear to others; at other times, we feel embarrassed by our behavior, our sinful thoughts, or our inability to function in the present. With our many losses of family members and our tiny children, we have noticed that there are similarities and differences in how we grieved each loss. Take some time to explore your own reactions to loss. If you have lost more than one relationship, do you see any patterns regarding your thoughts, feelings, or behavior?

The first time we lost a child, we worshiped as we sat in the emergency room. We cried. We hurt. Then we took nearly a year to allow ourselves to grieve before trying to get pregnant again. When we had another miscarriage again in 2016, we were devastated. We had guarded our hearts. We had waited to share our news with others. We felt like we had prepared for the battle ahead of us. But somehow we still felt completely unequipped for what we faced. This time, we had a traumatic experience in the emergency room with two cold hospital staff members. The hospital bed was not equipped with stirrups, so the staff used bedpans and blankets instead, leaving me, Ashley, in a physically and emotionally vulnerable position. They also refused us permission to see our baby on the screen. We felt overwhelmed, knowing it could be the last time we'd see our baby, yet our efforts were met with hostility and a callous explanation of protocol.

Over the course of several hours, we expected the worst but fought to be optimistic. Denial, optimism, and the dire reality of our past waged an internal war that sought to seize our emotional stability. As we stood in the hospital's frigid, sterile waiting room, an elderly lady passed us an antique, corded phone. Our doctor's voice stung with the dreaded news. "No, no, no," my voice echoed throughout the hospital. This was *not* the news we wanted. We wanted our child to live.

In the following weeks, we continued to pray and read God's Word, seeking His guidance for our family's future and the areas where we still maintained leadership roles. We felt powerless to save the child we never got to know. We felt that God was distant when we needed His comfort, silent when we were desperate for His voice.

With our third loss, our baby boy survived a little longer in the womb. We prepared in several additional ways, including visiting specialists, taking medications, and sharing our news with only a few family members after we were "far enough along" to feel that our baby's odds of survival were pretty good. This experience was much less traumatic regarding the hospital staff, but we had learned what to ask for *before* the visit. We continued to learn from our past hurts, but no matter how much we tried, there were novel ways of being wounded. This time the nurse allowed us to see the screen. We immediately saw that the baby's heart had become still. I, Ashley, whispered, "What happened to you, little guy?" I felt deflated. Hurt. Brokenhearted. I was angry that my body had rebelled against its duty to protect my child.

During that season, if I had been able to separate from myself, I may have physically duked it out with the part of me that had failed my child. I continued to take my hurt to God but repeatedly experienced deafening silence. At times, I wondered if God cared. I looked to God's Word and read between the lines. How did the characters feel about their connection to God? Did Moses feel like God was right by his side *all* the time? What about Joshua, the disciples, Paul?

We've been taught that there were periods of silence in Scripture. The lifetime of lessons we learned throughout our years of attending church, listening to sermons, and completing Bible courses reminded us that there is hope. We don't have to rely solely on our feelings. We'll take our feelings to the Father, knowing that He hears us. Even if we don't *always* feel close to Him, we know He's near. Though we felt His presence more during our first loss, He was equally present with each subsequent loss we faced.

Grief Affects Us in Unique Ways

We have faced other losses that we will discuss throughout our time together. But one of the biggest lessons we have learned is that grief looks different for each person. Even the same person experiencing similar losses can respond in new ways to each loss. When we face an experience repeatedly, we may be affected in surprising ways. But the *hope* that we have found is that we are resilient. We can keep growing, sharing, and fighting to overcome.

We continued to run to God with our sorrow. We picked each other up, prayed, and helped each other through the most awful moments.

As you think about your losses, process the ways your relationships have been impacted. Maybe you told yourself it's better to avoid close relationships because they leave you hurting. Grief is known for being a liar. Can you identify any lies you've been tempted to believe?

Grief Lies . . . But Also Reveals Some Truth

No person will ever completely understand what we have faced. Grief lies, telling us we are alone, but truly, we still need one another. Right now, when we're hurting, community is more important than ever. So we hope you'll prepare yourself for a journey. Determine to finish. You're a warrior. We are going to do some training. And in the end, you'll be stronger, more determined, and better able to rescue others whose breath has been taken by loss.

It may be beneficial to choose one experience of loss to focus on and then return to the content later with another encounter to process. If you have a friend or loved one who may be willing to embark on this journey with you, ask them. People want to feel needed. Your support system likely wants to help but doesn't know what you need, doesn't want to pressure you, or simply isn't skilled at helping someone who is grieving. It's okay to ask for help. In fact, it may help them too! Loss can feel overwhelming; taking time to examine various elements in bite-size pieces will help you heal and enable you to help someone else down the road.

Let's do this together.

seeing myself

How we see ourselves greatly impacts our lives. When we lose something or someone important to us, our confidence can take a blow. We may feel emotionally fatigued, out of control, or unable to think creatively. When we take time to look deeply at ourselves, especially our needs and expectations, we gain understanding about how to meet our needs in healthier ways. Invite God to help you explore any unwanted new titles you hold, identify defense mechanisms you use to aid in self-protection, and work through activities to increase understanding of yourself.

2 | the day everything changed

SOMETIMES EVERYTHING CHANGES in an instant. Other times, there is a slow progression toward a dreaded moment. When I found porn on Chuck's computer, I was crushed. Nothing would ever be the same again. You see, we had decided to wait until we were married to have sex. And it had been an overwhelmingly difficult task. We went to extremes, continuously readjusting our boundaries, learning that we would get too intimate when we were at Chuck's apartment alone. When I found the inappropriate images, my mind raced. I was devastated that he could allow himself to cheat, to sin against God, and to look at naked people when we were trying to save intimacy for each other.

Each of us has a mountain of trauma, broken relationships, or disappointments we can grieve. Or we can bury them. The truth is, we've all experienced unmet expectations. Things aren't what they're supposed to be. Sin entered the world, and daily, we face its consequences. Whether you lost a job or a beloved pet or have an estranged relationship, things have changed. Yet we can nearly see it in your eyes. You aren't giving up. You're not going to let the enemy win. You're going to look at grief and

19

look her square in the eye, because when you do, you may see love. You're grieving something or someone you loved.

Grief in Real Time

As we began writing this book, I, Chuck, got a call. My grandmother had breathed her last breath. I had been expecting the call; she was ninety-eight years old and in hospice care. But preparation didn't chase the experience of loss out the door. Thoughts flooded me of past experiences and future losses that I know will come. When we face loss, time stands still. Time speeds away. The past and the future come crashing together in a single crescendo. You may find yourself staring at a computer screen, wondering where the time has gone, yet meetings or other engagements might seem to last forever and require more mental effort than in the past.

That same morning, I waited for butter to melt as I prepared breakfast—a solid transformed into a liquid. Change. Thoughts of the past and future flooded my mind. Life had changed so much.

Today, I lost a title. I no longer have someone who will call me grandson.

I used to be <u>a grandson</u>. Some may argue that I'm *still* a grandson, but that day my heart was highly aware of the loss.

It can be difficult to balance between giving ourselves space to "feel" the loss and continuing on. What is true strength? If we let ourselves walk through this experience of grief, we may lose all productivity for the day. However, if we barrel through without stopping to process, will we yell at our kids later?

Give yourself space to contemplate your experience, to "go there." Consider grabbing a notebook (or a notes app on your phone), a Bible, and a writing utensil to record your thoughts as you process. What has led to this point? Let time move. Let time be still. Embrace the moment. Allow yourself to be present with your thoughts.

Where were you when you faced loss? Perhaps it was a flashbulb moment that you'll never forget, or maybe it approached like billowing fog. As you think about your grief experience, allow yourself to feel the love that you had for what you lost. Love allows us to embrace the good memories. Fear causes us to continuously ask, "Will this happen to me again?" And if we answer yes, we may choose to protect ourselves rather than face our fears. For now, let's explore love.

Identifying What We Miss Most

Consider what you loved about what used to be. Although it is tough to go there, it is important. It will be worth it. What do you miss about the life, the relationship, the love that used to be present? Be specific. If you lost a loved one due to death by suicide, think of the deep love you felt for the person and a specific occasion that was positive. If you lost someone due to divorce, remember something specific you liked about being in a relationship with them. Or maybe you're grieving the loss of your family structure, thinking, *We used to be a family*. Process what you loved about being a family. This may feel counterproductive, but unless we take time to understand *what* we loved, it will become increasingly more difficult to fully love in the future.

We have lost things we love, things we *still* need. But we have not lost love. In what ways are we surrounded by love today? Those are the elements that will help us through this disaster.

Since we are asking you to engage in this exercise, we decided to take a moment and reflect on some of our grief during the lockdown in 2020. During this season, we lost our ability to gather in groups. We loved some things about what used to be.

We loved the energy and sound of a roaring crowd, especially thundering worship at church.

We loved hugging family and being close to friends.

We loved visiting unique local shops filled with sights and smells that satisfied our senses and ushered in creative inspiration.

As we began to list what we loved, we paused. Our tears caused us to want to shut down the exercise. But then we remembered that this is likely going to be *your* experience too. So let's be brave together. We *can* take the difficult steps toward healing.

As we reflected on the things we loved about the past, we recognized a difference between those who choose to look back and those who refuse. The business leaders and individuals who pivoted refused to let their pain turn into long-term hurt or anger. Although we may have earned the right to be hurt, let's reflect on what we loved so we can develop a path toward meeting our current unmet need for connection, stability, or purpose.

> Although we may have earned the right to be hurt, let's reflect on what we loved so we can develop a path toward meeting our current unmet need for connection, stability, or purpose.

It is likely that you missed some friends and family early in the pandemic. How did you respond? Did you deny those feelings, or did you take time to learn a new technology or create a novel method for being together?

We saw people sitting outside one another's homes, talking through screen doors. A local magician hosted virtual birthday parties, and we participated in parades where people traveled through neighborhoods in their cars to show their love for others. Church leaders were innovative, gathering for drive-in worship experiences, creating chalk walks in their parking lots to help parents engage their kids in spiritual activities, and utilizing online technologies to further their reach.

By looking *at* our need for connection to friends, family, and the body of Christ, we become resourceful. But when we deny our needs or deficits, we are unable to see our only source of healing and love, which comes from Christ. During the pandemic, we also saw people choose to isolate at home for months, staying indoors and distancing themselves from people altogether. We see a similarity in this behavior to how people respond to grief. Some people choose to look at grief, determining to be resilient. Others shut out the world, feeling crushed and overwhelmed. Which way do you lean regarding your grief?

When we allow ourselves to reflect on the love we lost, we become more free to connect with others. We can appreciate love from others and can process.

Let's choose love.

Earlier we shared that I, Ashley, used to be <u>pregnant</u>. And I, Chuck, used to be <u>a grandson</u>.

There are so many other things we used to be. We could spend our days leaning into what we no longer have, or we can devote our finite energy toward becoming healthy, knowing it will make a difference in the lives of those around us. We desperately cling to love. Let's take a moment to direct our attention toward God, inviting Him into the middle of where we are.

God,
   I look to You. I want to thrive again, to love again, to run to You with my hurt. Fill me with love, my Healer.

                                    Amen.

3 | where I am now

SAY THE FOLLOWING STATEMENT with us: "I am here. I have survived up to this point. Today, I am going to look at my grief."

We have been wounded, and now we have a choice to make. We can grab a cloth and attempt to stop the bleeding, or we can deny that we have been injured. Let's apply pressure to the wound to stop the bleeding.

The first step in our grief work is to admit we have a problem. We will unpack the Three A's to Change. The first step is to become *aware*. Take a moment to be aware of the hurt you're experiencing. Invite God into the process; He will help you understand what's in your heart that leads you away from the path of life. Consider praying the words of David in Psalm 139:23–24:

> Search me, O God, and know my heart;
> test me and know my anxious thoughts.
> Point out anything in me that offends you,
> and lead me along the path of everlasting life.

After we have become aware of our hurt, we can *assess* what has and has not worked to ease the pain. We can also assess other options we hope to try in the future. The final step is to *act*. After we have processed our pain and the ways we have effectively and ineffectively worked to meet our needs, we can begin a new course of action. We will continue to apply the Three A's to Change throughout this book.

In our fast-paced world, we may refuse to look at our pain, but looking away does not stop the bleeding. Or we can labor feverishly at work or home, believing success will cauterize the wound. But we do not heal a hemorrhaging limb by building wealth or vacuuming floors. We must look directly at the injury to understand how to get better. There may be dirt that needs to be cleaned out. It could be painful. We have been hurt, yet we have survived. Facing the pain is the only way to rid us of our constant suffering. Denying its existence only further deepens the injury in the long run.

So today we begin. Or we begin again. We choose to look at our hurt, to go on a journey to find hope, to liberate ourselves of the dark cloud that has followed us for days, weeks, or years now.

Today, we look at our grief.

How have you been changed by grief?

Job Loss

In 2007, about two weeks before our wedding, Chuck and I started working at the same company. About a week later, I got let go! At the time, I could've filled in the blank by saying, "I used to be <u>employed</u>." This was devastating on so many levels, especially because it was my first degree-level job. Even as I write these words, I feel tempted to tell you all the reasons it wasn't my fault I was canned. But the truth is, I became defensive during the training process when Chuck and I were accused of doing something we didn't do. (Please ask what happened. I'm having a difficult time withholding the story!)

All right, you twisted my arm; I'll share the story. During training, about eight new employees were crammed into a closet-sized room that could barely fit a table. When we were waiting for the training to begin, an employee thought they saw us kiss. When I was called into the boss's office with the employee who had accused us of this heinous crime, I insisted that we did not kiss—because we didn't! It's amazing how the memory works. I cannot clearly recall what was said, but since I didn't admit to kissing, the owner said something to the effect of "I think it will be a good idea if we part ways. I'd be willing to consider having you return and work here down the road, but I think it would be best if we part ways for now."

I bawled. Our financial security was shaken. My pride was hurt. We had just moved, and our stability felt swept away. We had never experienced anything like that before.

All of us grieve so many things. Or we bury our grief. We grieve a job loss, the childhood we missed out on, rejections, lost relationships, and death. It seems that we easily ascribe the word *grief* to death but not to other losses. Who decided that? When we grieve, we experience intense emotion that results from losing something or someone that met a deep need within us.

Grief Thrusts Us into a Negative Space

A negative space is the intangible mental space where one's hopes and dreams about life seem to be lost. Consider if your grief changed you, moving you into a negative space. When we choose to begin new relationships, we usually start in a positive space, with many positive aspirations regarding the present and future. When those expectations go unmet and are disrupted by conflict, a cancer diagnosis, or unfaithfulness, we may be catapulted into a negative space.

Everyone wants to return to a positive space, but not everyone is able to find their way back. And sometimes people so badly want to be in a positive space, they will deny they are facing troublesome times to live under the facade that they are okay. This process of moving from a positive to a negative space and from a negative to a positive space is called Switch Theory. We will explore this concept throughout our time together to help you escape negative spaces in healthy ways.

Building Awareness

Take a moment to think about your thoughts. Consider what you have you been thinking about in the past twenty-four hours. Have your thoughts been overwhelmingly positive, negative, or somewhere in between? You could be living in a positive or a negative space, you might be bouncing back and

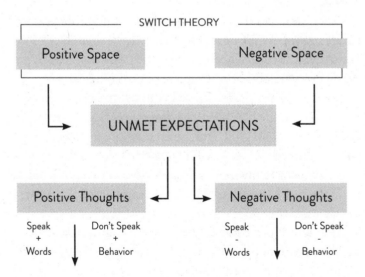

forth between both spaces, or you may be in a positive space with some people and in a negative space with others.

Now, let's explore how your thoughts impact your behavior. Do you tend to speak or remain quiet regarding your feelings, especially the negative ones? Many people remain quiet about issues until they've become so entrenched in a negative space that they explode or implode. But we see a better way. Our lives can be different if we find our way back to a positive space where we can communicate our unmet expectations in a healthy way. We will use the Three A's to Change to help with this process, starting with building awareness. First, rate the intensity of your grief.

1

low intensity

10

high intensity

Next, ask yourself, "How am I coping? What am I doing to survive?"

Everyone copes differently, but the common thread is that we *are* coping. We are doing our best to survive amid our hurt. Sometimes we cope in healthy ways, and other times, we choose momentary relief that can deplete our overall health.

Consider if you have allowed yourself to laugh, to cry, to _____. Fill in the blank with whatever you may have resisted doing as a result of guilt, fear, or exhaustion; process the ways you have coped. When I, Ashley, experienced my first miscarriage, we went to my mom's house. Mom combed my hair as I laid my head on her lap. I fell asleep and woke up crying. It wasn't a bad dream. It was our reality.

After one of our babies passed away a couple of years later, we played with our other kids in the front yard. We remember having so many emotions. But we continued to move—not because it was easy but because we had little ones who wanted to play. We didn't want to lose more moments with them because of being sad. And they were hurting too. Cheering them up made us feel a little better. These were positive coping mechanisms we used. One of the negative coping mechanisms we used was creating relational distance. We found that if we spent time with people, we felt drained; they would offer unhelpful words, or they would most commonly avoid the subject altogether. The latter was the worst.

When I lost my job, I coped positively by crying and later by hustling and juggling several part-time jobs. I taught at a private Christian high school and instructed fitness classes at a local gym, and we became marriage educators.

When I, Chuck, confessed to looking at pornography, I coped positively by setting up accountability with a mentor and a close friend. Being confronted with my shame pushed me to get honest about a battle I had been fighting alone. I needed to let this hurt draw me closer to God and Ashley through a more honest relationship with both of them, as well as with myself. When trust is broken, it may be tempting to cope by refusing to trust again. This may protect us in one sense, but it also inadvertently protects against love.

Our coping mechanisms are unique to our personalities, environment, abilities, and current situation. Let's explore some grief coping mechanisms. Take a moment to think of some positive and negative ways of coping. Process why we engage in negative forms of coping. We aren't *really* trying to hurt ourselves. We just want to feel better, which is a good thing. However, some coping mechanisms lead to more pain.

Let's walk this out. When we face loss, some of us push people away. We do this to cope. We feel hurt by what they say and upset by what they don't say. Our needs are unpredictable and bringing someone else into the mess feels complicated. We may not like ourselves a whole lot when we are around others as a result of feeling a loss of self-control. We are also gravely aware of how people leave us. So we struggle alone. When we suffer alone, we set ourselves up for future pain.

Sometimes we cope by distancing from God. Perhaps we feel shameful or undesirable because of our negative coping. We're allowed to admit disappointment, to feel hurt, to struggle with anger. But let's take it all to God. He's big enough to handle our deepest, darkest emotions and hurts. If you're in a negative space with God, tell Him about it. It may very well be your first step back toward a positive space.

As you think about how you cope, consider the *purpose* of coping. Coping allows us to feel happy again or prevents us from feeling unhappy (temporarily). For example, if we avoid talking about our loss, we momentarily keep ourselves from feeling sad. But, in time, avoidant behavior may end up leaving us feeling depressed and isolated. At first glance, avoiding communication may feel like a positive coping mechanism when in actuality, staying silent may bring about hurt and loneliness.

Each of us has positive and negative coping mechanisms that help in either the short or long term. Some positive coping mechanisms include crying, seeking community, or speaking with a pastor, counselor, or coach. We can give back, seek new adventures, or commit to prayer. Some negative coping mechanisms include sleeping excessively, self-medicating, isolating, engaging in risky behavior, and shutting God out.

Take time to list your positive and negative coping mechanisms. Then identify the "good" you're hoping to find as a result of your behavior.

Review the behaviors you listed. What needs are fulfilled with each one? If you cope with loss by taking a walk, consider how that helps you. Likely, walking helps you feel positively about yourself and gives you space to contemplate your desires,

EXAMPLE

Positive Coping Mechanisms	Negative Coping Mechanisms
· Allowing myself to feel · Community · Talking to a counselor or coach · Giving back · Prayer or meditation · New adventures	· Sleeping for days · Self-medicating · Isolation · Pushing people away · Extreme and risky behavior · Denial · Emotional disregard for physical health

Positive Coping Mechanisms	Negative Coping Mechanisms

and walking outside helps you connect to God and others you may pass by, which can meet some relational needs also. Are the behaviors making you happy, building joy? Many positive coping mechanisms involve facing the loss, while most of the negative behaviors are avoidant in nature. There are many other behaviors, some of which could be positive or negative. For example, working could be a positive coping mechanism if you are in a solid mental state. But if you lost your spouse last night, today is not a day to go to work. Doing so would likely be a negative coping mechanism. The answer to whether the action is a positive or negative coping mechanism lies in the reasoning for the behavior. Think about why you choose each behavior and how it makes you feel. For example, the behavior may help you avoid facing a painful reality or it may offer support and connection.

Reflect on your list of positive and negative coping mechanisms. Did you gain insight into the short-term benefits of your negative coping mechanisms? Pray about your behavior, asking God to meet your needs and provide understanding about your attempts to care for yourself. Pray about *each* positive and negative coping tool. Invite God into your mental space, asking Him to show you areas where you may be living in a negative space. Look for a correlation between days when you're in a positive space and days when you choose positive coping mechanisms.

God wants to walk alongside us, and He will reveal new methods we can try to meet our needs. In time, He may even help us understand our behavior in new ways. You may have heard of the saying "Time heals." But what we do with our time makes all the difference. Time spent engaging in negative coping can further deteriorate our view of God, ourselves, and others.

You have survived. You are coping. We've explored some ways to build awareness regarding the positive and negative space; now, let's assess where we are when we communicate. We communicate from a positive or a negative space.

Assessing Our Communication Patterns

Now that we've gone through a process to understand our coping mechanisms, let's explore our communication habits. When you face unmet expectations, do you tend to speak up or stay quiet? Consider reviewing the Switch Theory graphic on page 27 to consider which tendency is most common for you. In the past, when you have spoken about your needs, have you done so from a positive or negative space? If you're complaining, you're communicating from a negative space. When you speak respectfully, sharing calmly about your unmet expectations and asking what you'd like to change, you're speaking from a positive space.

It's easy to start off a conflict conversation in a positive space and get triggered to a negative space. Contemplate where you are when you communicate about important issues. If you recall times when you have stayed quiet and spoken up from a positive and negative space, we recommend making a list identifying how you've communicated from each space. Look for themes. When have you been most successful at speaking from a positive space? Consider the time of day when you are more likely to speak from a negative space. There may be additional themes you notice as well. Having an "audience" may escalate frustrations more quickly, and bringing up conflict when you're tired may be a sign that you're waiting until you're in a negative space to talk or that you need to set time aside when you're more rested.

Now that you've processed what you're like when *you* experience unmet expectations, let's go deeper. When *others* speak with you about their unmet expectations, do they tend to stay quiet or speak from a positive or a negative space? We are greatly impacted by others' communication habits. It is important to recognize if others are communicating from a negative space because they will likely influence how you communicate also. Be careful not to shove *all* the blame onto them, however. If you notice that they are bringing up issues from a negative space, you can redirect or pause the conversation until each of you can communicate from a positive space.

Sometimes we may find it easy to communicate from a positive space, and other times it may feel like our mood or one particular person triggers us to communicate from a negative space. Regardless, our goal should be to communicate more frequently from a positive space. If you made a list of times you communicated from a positive and negative space, review the list and begin to develop a communication improvement plan. If you noticed that you communicate from a positive space most frequently when you're face-to-face with someone rather than communicating via text messaging, then create a mental checklist for yourself to go through before bringing up an issue. For example, maybe you want to tell a close friend you feel hurt that they haven't reached out regarding your loss and you're wondering why they've been so distant. If you realized many of your negative-space conversations began over text, determine not to start any of these types of conversations that way again. Consider asking the following questions to gain insight into yourself:

- What themes have I discovered regarding my negative-space conversations?
- What themes have I discovered regarding my positive-space conversations?
- What items need to be part of my mental checklist to ensure that I communicate my needs and wishes from a positive space?

Act

Finally, now that you know when you are in a positive or a negative space, it's time for action. Be curious. Be patient. Try not to put too much pressure on yourself to be perfect. The goal is to continue to understand how good communication occurs. There are patterns, themes, and habits to explore. Your relationships are important and deserve attention. Keep up the great work. If you can communicate about your grief, you're gaining skills that many have yet to master. You can lead the way so that others will feel more equipped to talk about their hurts too.

God,

Help me identify when I'm in a negative space so I can get out! I invite You into the middle of my grief. Please make me aware of the ways I can grow. Give me the courage to think of new methods to try and the boldness to act in new ways.

Amen.

4 | naming my grief

IT'S TIME TO NAME what you lost. It may seem unnecessarily obvious. But there's power in identifying your loss. If you take time to identify the good things you are missing, you will be able to mourn, heal, and then look for new areas of purpose. Take a moment to pray. Tell God, "I am grieving _____, and I need Your help to heal."

Perhaps you are grieving the loss of stability, the loss of a loved one, or the loss of your identity.

When I, Chuck, was about to leave for college, I needed to grieve some things but didn't know it. I'd never had a huge passion for animals, but there I was, yelling about the lack of care I witnessed. A neighbor's dog was in a dirty kennel in the backyard with no water. Suddenly, anger came over me, and I didn't understand where it had come from. Because of my extensive expertise as a dog caretaker (just kidding, I had never owned or cared for a dog), I was filled with a righteous animal rights anger that I'm sure PETA would have been proud of. I called a friend, not the dog's owner, and complained about the animal's living conditions; I rattled on about how I wanted to rescue the dog and take him to the vet. My friend was completely thrown off and promptly told me to calm down.

Looking back, I see that I was scared. I was afraid I wouldn't be successful in college and this life change would be more than

I could handle. I didn't know it at the time, but I was grieving the anticipated loss of the comfort and security I loved. I had always identified as someone who had everything together. Life was changing, and I didn't know how to handle it. Like many of us do, I used anger to express what I didn't know how to communicate any other way. I was angry about how the dog was treated, but if I had truly been angry about its treatment, I would've filled a jug with water and taken care of the dog's basic needs. Instead, I complained to a friend, never speaking to the dog's owner.

Can you relate? Not knowing what is going on inside our hearts and minds can lead us to feel like we are a bit out of control. Going to difficult emotional places helps us identify what we're grieving and leads us to build self-awareness and self-regulation. This awareness enables us to process in a healthier way. What if this work could prevent future hurt and wounds?

Soon after this incident, I went to college. By the end of the first semester, I had crashed. I was a poor student and flunked out. Maybe I had known I wasn't ready. What if I had gone to that place of fear and grief when I became overwhelmed with anger regarding the neighbor's dog? What if I had asked myself, "Is this what I'm really concerned about?" Would that emotional work have freed me up to become successful academically? If I had taken the time to name what I was grieving, I'm pretty sure things would have been different. Instead, my anger was displaced onto the dog's owner, and I buried my fears about the future.

Identifying Our Grief

When we faced recurrent miscarriage, we grieved the loss of life and also our hopes and dreams. We were saddened because we did not want our little ones to lose their lives. But we were also devastated that our dreams were dashed. As we allowed ourselves to look at our hurt, we were able to pinpoint our most vulnerable places.

Naming the grief that resulted from Chuck's pornography use was also powerful for us. I, Ashley, grieved <u>a loss of trust</u>. This is something I began grieving on day 1 and still grieve today. Still, though it's been over fifteen years, I sometimes feel a need to investigate, even though Chuck's behavior has seemed honorable. At times, trust comes easily, and other times, it's okay to trust, ask questions, and investigate at the same time. We are thankful for mercy from our Father. Both of us need grace to be accepted by God, so we work to continue building a safe and trustworthy space for each other where we can be honest about our weaknesses.

What areas of your life have been impacted by loss? When our dreams are dashed in one area of our lives, purpose wanes in other areas as well. It is quite difficult to be full of vision in one area when we feel lifeless in another. To be whole, we must look at our entire self.

I am grieving
_____.

Take a moment to fill in the blank for yourself. I am grieving _____. Maybe you will write down several items. Then think about the love that came before your grief.

We may think we will feel better in the future if we stop loving now, but the absence of love does *not* bring happiness. Do you feel tempted to stifle love, imagining that blocking out love will protect you in some way? When people contemplate suicide, they often report having a difficult time imagining that life could feel joyful in the future. They are in a negative space with the world. We have all been in a negative space. We have experienced unmet expectations and told ourselves we will work on it tomorrow, thinking we will feel more motivated then. We think we can predict how we will feel in the future, but we struggle to accurately predict our emotions. We are poor predictors of our future emotions. However, we can look at the past and learn from it. If we find ourselves imagining the future as a dark place, it may be an indication that we are in a negative space. We can look at our wounds, acknowledge that we need help, and learn how to escape negative spaces.

At times, people in deep grief may choose to stay in bed for days, telling themselves they will surely feel better if they sleep a bit more. But if we stay in bed today, waiting to do the hard work tomorrow, we will have missed out on the opportunity to build strength. And tomorrow, we will likely repeat this thought cycle, pushing off the activity yet another day. The attempt to predict our future emotions is called affective forecasting. We may not always be the best at predicting our future emotions, but we can get better through building awareness. We may *think* our efforts to forego love will protect us, but in the end, doing so is our kryptonite.

> We are poor predictors of our future emotions.

As you reflect on your personal journey, explore the following question: Other than getting back what I lost, what do I need now? As you explore the emotions you have experienced, you may get overwhelmed. Do not feel the need to examine every one of them at once. As you reflect on your needs, start small. Consider making a list of your "met" and "unmet" needs. Who could you ask to help you meet *one* need?

How Has Grief Impacted My Emotional Stability

In 2017, after facing losses in each of the two preceding years, we were emotionally spent. We felt alone, vulnerable. At times, we could not handle our kids' fighting, and we found it taxing to engage with people who were unintentionally insensitive to our experiences. To cope, we pulled back socially. We even grieved that our support system was not what we needed it to be.

After several "out of character" encounters (this is a nice way to describe our "explosive behavior," which we will discuss later), we decided to ask for what we needed. We needed someone to listen to us. One person we hoped would listen was known for being a talker but was someone we loved and trusted. So we asked them to come to our home and *just* listen. It was vulnerable to ask but felt empowering afterward. They listened, and we felt a little better that day.

We can grieve simple things such as walking into church as a family, having someone who regularly asks us about our day, or the birthday party that we should be planning for a loved one who has passed. We can grieve that we used to be "bubbly," and we can be angry with ourselves for the ways our identity seems to be wrapped up in a relationship or job title.

When Robert lost his job, he realized his work mattered more than he'd thought. He grieved the ways his success at work built him up and gave him a sense of value that was now missing. Let's also consider Sandra's grief. Two weeks after Sandra had an abortion, she was filled with regret and found it difficult to find joy in everyday tasks. Sandra grieved that she'd felt pressured to end her baby's life, and she grieved her decision to glance away from the screen rather than looking at her little one's moving fingers and toes. Finally, she also grieved that she suffered alone because she told no one about this decision.

As we identify our grief, we recognize our losses. We see our reflection in a mirror. Our view of ourselves often changes because of our loss. For a season, we thought we were strong. After facing loss, we saw so much weakness in ourselves. As we define our grief and the unmet needs that are exposed, we can begin to pick up the pieces. As we name our grief, we can see our wounds that need bandaging and can invite God into the restoration process.

> God,
>
> Give me the courage to name what I am grieving, to look at my losses and ultimately look to You for help. I need You more than I need breath, more than I need my physical or emotional needs met. Fill me with You.
>
> Amen.

5   unwanted new title

LOSS HAS A WAY of gifting us with unwanted titles. Unemployed, barren, addict, widow, divorced, orphan, single. None of us want to be labeled, yet these titles exist.

As we look at ourselves and explore what lies beneath, we may feel a sting, like we are cleaning out a wound. Take a moment to process which new unwanted title you have been granted through this tragedy. Ask yourself, "Who am I now? Who have I become?" Answering these questions can be painful. But if we never take time to examine ourselves closely, someday we may not leave the legacy we once hoped we would leave.

Gaining the title of widow, orphan, or divorced may leave us feeling alone, unknown. These unwanted titles can be difficult to accept, so give yourself permission to avoid using them if you'd like. And feel free to ask a few members of your support system to avoid using these terms if it helps. Let's explore some of the reasons unwanted titles feel so painful.

1. We have never identified ourselves in this way, so it feels foreign.
2. These are terms that identify us based on our brokenness rather than our strengths.

3. We may have previously and unintentionally looked down on someone in one of these groups, feeling sorry for them or ascribing weakness to them.

4. We do not like to be stereotyped or placed in boxes or categories, and this new, stereotyped title is a reminder of how our identity has changed.

Do you identify with any of the reasons above? If so, give yourself space to share how you feel with a loved one, counselor, or friend.

Earlier, I shared that I recently lost the title of grandson. As I accepted this change, I was able to look at what I loved about being a grandson. Simply distracting or ignoring the topic as a protective mechanism would not have helped me process or heal.

But it's not always just titles that are difficult to swallow. Overall, many grief terms can feel insensitive or simply not enough to sum up the intensity of emotion we experience.

When I, Ashley, began researching treatment options for myself during our season of loss, I discovered that I did not care for the sterile medical terms that were used (recurrent miscarriage, spontaneous abortion, secondary infertility, etc.). Terms and titles don't have to define us, but they can still be painful.

If we break down the term *miscarriage*, it sounds like a "misstep" in the way I "carried" our baby. Amid grief, the term may not carry enough weight for the amount of pain parents experience. For a while, I wouldn't even use the term. Instead, I would say, "My baby died." Changing the language we used was empowering for us.

What terms sting right now? If there are people who use these terms in conversation with you, consider sharing with them how the words feel foreign or unwanted or are constant reminders of who you do not want to be. This should help you feel seen.

We, in time, came to feel less triggered when we heard the word *miscarriage*. In fact, now we can use it without feeling the full extent of our hurt. How will you feel next week or next year? We cannot say for sure because we are poor predictors of our future emotions, and predicting others' emotions can be even more difficult. But we found that giving ourselves permission to avoid painful terms helped us. The more we consider our needs, the easier it becomes to share them with others, ask for what we want, and meet them.

Other Unwanted Titles

When Cho's wife died suddenly, he sat in shock, saying, "I cannot believe I'm a widower." Later, he kept repeating to himself and others, "Me? I'm a widower? How did this happen?" He didn't need someone to explain what had occurred. He outwardly shared an internal dissonance he faced. Without warning, his entire life changed. His title changed. His future changed. His identity changed. With one title change, he experienced an onslaught of unmet expectations.

Dissonance: mental tension that results when expectations and reality do not line up.

Consider another scenario. Ada found herself explaining how she was not like a typical divorcée. As she shared with us the story of becoming a single mother, she expressed disbelief, confusion, and other dissonant emotions. She had a difficult time accepting her new, unwanted title. Therefore, she took every opportunity to explain herself to others. "My husband cheated on me, and I had no idea it was going on. I left for the sake of the kids." She was certain to share the story in a manner that made her feel unique. *I am not like them*, she'd think to herself. Does this sound anything like my need to explain the story behind getting fired? Both Ada and I felt labeled, and when we didn't identify with the new stereotypical labels we were assigned, we experienced dissonance.

I didn't identify with many of the characteristics I had previously heard about others who were fired. Those I knew who had been terminated had shown up late or stolen money from the organization or hadn't worked hard.

When we face dissonance, our minds try to reconcile the new information, so if Ada had previously judged someone who was divorced, she likely needed to perform mental gymnastics to protect herself from self-judgment. Sometimes our minds are so desperate to feel okay that we distort our experiences to preserve our view of ourselves. Perhaps Ada *was* different from these individuals. Either way, it takes courage, but we can explore the origins of the painful title. Why is this title triggering so much strife? A *trigger* is a stimulus that evokes a strong emotional response. As we understand the source of the hurt, we can begin to work toward neutralizing the trigger.

Neutralizing Triggers

How do we neutralize our triggers? Though this process takes time and we may not be able to completely neutralize every trigger, we can make progress. Rather than running away or avoiding situations where we may be triggered, we can lean in, seek understanding, and work to change our thinking and behavior.

Again, we will use the Three A's to Change. The first step is to become *aware* of your triggers. Write them down, then think about the experiences that have stimulated the strongest responses in you. Are there specific people, places, or things that have triggered overwhelm? Have you ever dealt with this?

For example, consider if you have spoken to the individual and directly asked them to speak or behave differently.

After building awareness, the next two steps are to *assess* and then *act*. Let's consider Melissa's situation. Her father was accused of sexual misconduct with some children in the neighborhood and she wondered if she might have been a victim as well; though she didn't remember the incident, years later, she smelled his shaving cream and was triggered. The smell of the cream evoked thoughts of her dad, and then she lost her appetite and began to shake. Melissa says she doesn't really want to know what happened with her father, and she has spent most of her life trying to avoid thinking about him. A potential title Melissa is working to avoid is *childhood sexual assault victim*. You can imagine why she may want to push this title out of her consciousness, possibly even repressing some of her past, hoping to make it "go away." In addition to the unwanted title, the amount of dissonance she would face in relation to her father and mother is excruciating. But avoiding this topic has created land mines that are in danger of being detonated during conversations, upon exposure to scents, or when visiting specific locations.

One step Melissa can take is to increase *awareness* of her triggers by talking with a counselor or friend about both positive and negative experiences during her childhood. Then she can explore triggers and *assess* ways to respond. For example, she can brainstorm options that could help neutralize her triggers. One method is to continue talking about the topic that brings overwhelm. Our bodies habituate as we talk about difficult topics, meaning that our heart rate may lower and we may feel safer to explore unmet needs if we share in a safe space. Other options include speaking with her father, writing a letter that she keeps for herself, or adjusting her boundaries in her other relationships. As we explore Melissa's triggers, we can continue to help her implement new, healthier ways to meet her needs. After we've assessed some options, it's time to move to the third A, to *act*.

As you reflect on your unwanted titles and triggers, take time to increase your awareness regarding how you have coped, assess new strategies to try, and begin acting in new ways. Though avoiding some situations may be natural in the beginning, ignoring triggers doesn't neutralize them; it typically allows them to secretly grow stronger. If we do not deal with our triggers, they will likely show up in unsuspecting places and cause a reaction that will remind us of our wounds.

Must We Accept a New Title?

We've not met anyone who instantly liked a new title associated with loss. If you've struggled to accept a new title, you're not alone. If you've experienced no problem slipping into a new uniform, then congratulations. You're likely in the minority. However you feel about it, take a moment to examine the "why" behind your feelings. Let your emotions teach you. Don't let them be in charge, but emotions can be powerful teachers. After all, God designed our emotions as an alert system. Each one notifies us about different stimuli. Some emotions, like anger, can be quite complex. For example, if we feel angry because we see a teenager picking on a first grader, we may be alerted to protect that innocent child. However, we can also feel angry about someone's lack of communication, a person speeding past us on the highway, or a child who doesn't show as much respect as we feel should be shown. In each of these angry situations, we may experience different alerts or emotions based on how we were created, our values, and even our mood. Most of us want people to communicate well, drive safely, and treat others with respect. If we invest time into understanding why specific emotions are triggered within us, we will gain insight into our values.

Our strongest emotions reveal our deepest values. If we've moved to a negative space, it's because we first were in a positive space. We valued something, and it was threatened. Our expectations were not met, but we can look at the emotions, titles, and hurt, seeking to submit all our internal commotion to the Lord who helps us learn, ask for what we need, and heal from brokenness. Even when we overreact to a situation with a neighbor's dog, we can explore what emotions have been triggered and why. I, Chuck, experienced strong emotions regarding the dog; that doesn't necessarily mean I deeply value dogs. It's important to be curious, inviting yourself to wonder why you're experiencing such strong emotions and what values might be threatened. We can ask if this response serves as a distraction from what is weighing on our mind or if it triggers something deeper within us. Perhaps I was creating drama about the neighbor's dog to distract myself from my ambiguity about college, or perhaps I experienced a low frustration tolerance because I wasn't facing my uncertainty about moving away or growing up. Taking time to explore the relationship between emotions and values can be quite revealing.

> Our strongest emotions reveal our deepest values.

No one can make us accept an unwanted title. It is up to us to decide. Will the new title help us connect with others who are in a similar situation? Does the new title sting? Quite possibly. But as we explore, we will continue to grow and understand what's beneath our strongest feelings.

God,

In my hurt, I remind myself that my role as a child of God is more important than any other title I may be assigned by humans. I give You my titles, the ones I dislike and the ones I wish I still held. I look to You for renewed purpose. Fill me with love.

Amen.

6 | giving myself permission to grieve

IF YOU HAVE BEEN to more than one funeral in your lifetime, you have probably noticed some differences. Sometimes the family is strong, asking people how *they* are, smiling, and engaging with others. Other times, the grief is like smog—so thick that breathing feels impossible. Consider what makes some people able to carry on while others crumble.

Somehow you've formed a belief regarding how you expect yourself to look in your grief. You've developed beliefs about appropriate and inappropriate grief. Explore how you formed these beliefs and expectations. Maybe you feel pressured by culture or believe you should behave similarly to family members.

Who Told You How to Grieve?

So much of what guides us is internal. Consider who or what guides your internal voice. Are you allowed to cry? Men are often expected to be strong, so they may not feel the freedom to express themselves through tears. Or perhaps crying was the only acceptable emotional expression in your family. Maybe you're unwilling to let yourself feel because you've lost control in the past or have been taunted for your feelings. These may be valid reasons to avoid letting yourself experience hurt, but do you really want someone else's uncaring response or your past mistakes to keep you from healing?

You loved. You were loved. Without love (or at least the expectation that love is a possibility), there isn't a strong sense of loss. Give yourself permission to feel, to laugh, to _____. How do you fill in the blank? I give myself permission to _____.

If you filled in the blank with a negative term, such as *leave*, *scream*, or *hate*, or if you filled in the blank with a more positive idea, let's explore *why* giving yourself permission could be helpful, even if your behavior is less than ideal.

> I give myself
> permission to
> _____.

Why should we give ourselves permission to feel? Permission empowers. Locking away our feelings often imprisons us and prevents us from moving to a place where we can laugh and experience loving feelings when we reflect on our past.

In a year or two, who do you want to be? Are there unhealthy expectations placed on you that keep you from processing your hurt? If so, think about who put them on your shoulders. For example, suppose an aunt kindly asked you how you are and then said, "Hopefully you'll feel better in a month or two." When you feel terrible later, you might think, *You should be feeling better by now.* Instead of simply accepting those negative feelings, give yourself permission to release the expectations that you and others have put on yourself and say, "Grief is unpredictable. I give myself permission to be wrong about my assumptions regarding how long it will take to heal."

Or let's imagine that you complete the sentence by saying, "I give myself permission to lie in bed all day." Take some time to reflect on *why* it's healthy to give yourself permission to do so. Exploring *why* will help you identify if it's an appropriate or even truly desirable act.

It's possible that taking a day to recover from the emotional trauma you've faced is exactly what you need. But let's explore some of the reasons people may lie in bed day after day.

1. Loss of purpose
2. Desire to pass the time
3. Overwhelm—every time you wake up, you feel overwhelmed and want to escape into another slumber
4. Fear
5. Emotional or physical exhaustion (this can result from your body using adrenaline for an extended period)

Exploring the why provides insight that can inform us how to act. If we want to sleep to escape, let's identify what we're escaping from and what need is being met by staying in bed. When we face our fears, we gain power. When we run from them, we may fatigue ourselves until we fall.

Give Yourself Permission to *Feel* and *Behave* Differently with Each Loss

Understanding our needs can be challenging. And who can truly explain exactly *why* we do what we do? We can gain insight through reflection, learning from others, and exploring our own past experiences, but as much as we wish they would, these things will not give us full control over our future behavior.

One reason we try to avoid feeling is to prevent future pain. If we give ourselves permission to feel, we open ourselves up to being hurt again. This leaves us vulnerable and can be frightening. Each loss impacts us differently and causes us to behave in varying ways. In fact, each day we face the same loss may impact us in unique ways, triggering unusual behavior. As we give ourselves permission to be curious about our feelings rather than hiding them, we will become better equipped to meet our needs in healthy ways.

As we shared before, with each of our losses, we felt differently. We had shifting needs, and our perspectives were altered. When we faced our third loss, one of our strongest feelings was a sense of distance from God. We continued to ask God questions and look to Scripture for situations where people felt like He didn't *see* them. Did you know David felt distant from God? He prayed, "How long, LORD? Will you forget me forever? How long will you hide your face from me?" (Ps. 13:1 NIV). If David was called a man after God's own heart (1 Sam. 13:14), yet even he experienced times of distance from God, then we are okay. Did you hear me? Try reading it out loud. We are okay. If this psalm resonated with you, consider listening to Shane and Shane's song titled "Psalm 13."[1]

In Isaiah 55:8, God says, "For my thoughts are not your thoughts, neither are your ways my ways" (NIV). In verse 9, God shares that His thoughts are higher than our own. We don't have to understand why God chooses to be silent at times; we can still put our faith in Him, trusting that His thoughts and motives are better than ours.

> We don't have to understand why God chooses to be silent at times; we can still put our faith in Him, trusting that His thoughts and motives are better than ours.

Understanding that David felt unseen helped us feel a little bit less alone and freed us to contemplate our deeper feelings.

If David made it into the pages of Scripture and he felt distant from God, we can rest believing that God is still sovereign and feeling abandoned doesn't mean we are. Psalm 34:18 says, "The LORD is close to the brokenhearted and saves those who are crushed in spirit" (NIV). We can stand on God's Word. Since His Word tells us He is near, He is.

If all those words didn't break through the hurt you feel, consider permitting yourself to explore the walls of pain that separate you from God.

Permission to Be Angry with God

You can give yourself permission to be angry with God. If this doesn't settle well with you, think of your closest relationships. Have you grown upset with people from time to time? Yes. You are separate individuals with unique interests and expectations, and you're close enough to share those desires rather than keep them to yourself. Though God is all-knowing, we are not. We can become angry that God did not save our marriage, our job, or our loved one from tragedy. He could have intervened. And that hurts.

And it's okay that it hurts.

But when we tell God He should have done it our way, aren't we kind of insisting that we know better than He does? His ways are higher; we don't see the whole picture. God sees into heaven. He also sees all the sin. And He made the choice to give us free will. He deeply understands the outcomes of all the options we have thought of. And for reasons we are not able to contemplate, sometimes He chooses not to intervene.

When we read Scripture and see the number of people who were martyred, we ask this same question. Why God? Why do You allow suffering when You have the authority to make it stop?

We are certain we do not understand completely, but we have noticed that God has been disappointed with human suffering, and it pains Him to see sin and sorrow steal so much from His children (Gen. 18:20–21; Isa. 63:9). God often spoke directly or through prophets or angels to help us understand that He wants to be near and to give us direction regarding how to restore our relationship with Him and others. One reason God wrote the Ten Commandments is to help us understand what specific actions create distance between us and Him. When we are jealous or angry, for example, we can hurt ourselves, our relationships with others, and ultimately, our relationship with God (Exod. 20:17).

When we face moments when we feel unseen by God, we recall that one of the many names of God is "El Roi," which means the God who sees me.[2] We believe God's Word and use it to speak truth over our disbelief, hurt, or despair.

We can deduce the following statements even though our feelings may not always lead us to believe them:

1. God is present because His Word tells us He is.
2. God doesn't want much of the suffering that exists in the world. One day, He will redeem what has been lost.

So go ahead and give yourself permission to feel. Perhaps it will free you.

Don't Give Yourself Permission to Do This

We believe there are many unhelpful ways people could give themselves permission. For example, we do not want to give ourselves permission to sin. If you filled in the blank by giving yourself permission to throw a brick through someone's window, it may cause more harm than good. But we can still explore this idea in order to help you see why we don't want to give ourselves permission to do whatever we want. Likely, anyone who does such an act has been hurt and is attempting to redeem a sense of power or justice from the situation. Even when we do wrong, we receive some (often momentary) benefit from the behavior. Good can be found in every bad choice. There is function in every dysfunctional behavior. When we explore the good in our bad behavior, we are empowered to meet our needs in a healthier way. For example, if you gave yourself permission to throw a brick, the function in the dysfunctional behavior might be to show someone that they should stop hurting you because you will stand up for yourself. Now that you've identified the function in the dysfunction, you can look for other, *legal* ways to meet your needs. Perhaps you could speak directly to the person, knowing that if you do not speak, you may find yourself fantasizing about more dramatic, possibly incriminating options.

Other Questions to Explore

This loss has impacted you, making you stronger or weaker. It's left you with unmet expectations, and reflection is a powerful tool to help you gain clarity regarding your needs and desires. One of the most important roles we have found as a counselor and pastor is to help people think deeply through reflection. Consider discussing the following questions with a loved one.

1. *Have you given yourself permission to accept that your initial mental timeline regarding how you would feel may have been off? If it has taken you longer to heal than you first believed, it's all right to adjust those expectations rather than be angry with yourself.*

2. *What experiences or feelings do you need to give yourself permission to face?* Whether you're facing the inability to focus at work, overwhelm, or difficulty listening to other people's problems, you're not alone in your feelings and experiences.

3. *Do you find yourself comparing your grief expression to others?* Giving yourself and your loved ones permission to grieve differently is liberating. Consider why it may be difficult to allow others to grieve as they wish. Their strength or strong emotion can induce guilt related to your personal expression of loss.

Lee was angry that his family wanted to talk about his wife who had recently passed. He didn't want to. When he processed why he felt angry with his family, he realized he was trying to protect himself from feeling sad so he could work. As he looked beneath the surface, he let go of his frustration and gave his family permission to grieve on their own terms.

If you find yourself struggling with your healing timeline or comparing your grief to others, be curious about it. Ask God to help you understand what is being triggered. We've noticed that people frequently ask things like "How long was he sick?" "How far along were you?" or "Did you have any idea she was having an affair?" These questions are sometimes innocent, so it's okay to offer mercy to the individuals who ask them. But we have asked ourselves why we get so frustrated with these types of questions. It seems that people are trying to decide how much empathy to offer based on their comparison to other situations they've seen or experienced. Or at least, that's what we felt. If we answer that our loved one was sick for years, we may get less sympathy and a comment pointing to how it was good that we had time to say goodbye. We have found it better to avoid asking these types of questions and instead allow the person to share details they feel comfortable sharing.

Go ahead. Give yourself permission to process your hurts, bringing God into your negative spaces. He is your Redeemer.

> God,
>
> Give me confidence in who I am in You, not my ability to understand everything right now. Show me how to face and accept who I am in You above my current emotions.
>
> Amen.

7 exploring defense mechanisms

IT CAN FEEL EXCRUCIATING to face our losses. It may even feel more desirable to eat an entire roll of tinfoil than to look at our grief. All jokes aside, if we find it difficult to embrace our loss, there's a strong chance we've used some defense mechanisms to cope. A defense mechanism is a protective tool used to guard oneself from pain.[1] These defense mechanisms offer a form of protection, sheltering us from reality and wrapping us in an illusion of safety.

We may deny that the loss is real. We may disperse our strong emotions on an undeserving or safer source. Or we may make excuses for our behavior. We will explore some defense mechanisms a little more closely. Our goal is to help you identify dysfunctional ways of coping and replace them with healthier methods.

Denial

When we sense we may be losing someone or something we love, denial is quite common. This is the result of a painful reality. We may experience shock and operate on autopilot for a spell. We may push the issue out of our consciousness, hoping that the roaring laughter on the television will numb us. If someone is afraid their spouse is engaging in an inappropriate relationship, it might feel safer to look away because of a desire to avoid conflict, fear, or financial insecurity.

With our second loss, when I, Ashley, cried out at the hospital, I faced an inability to accept the news the doctor had shared through that ancient corded telephone; I was in a state of denial. We thought there was no way this could be happening again. We wanted desperately to prep the nursery and keep going with our plans to take this baby home from the hospital. Even though we had guarded ourselves in case we faced such a heartbreaking reality again, our attempts to stay distant from our emotions didn't make the moment hurt any less.

Once we feel safe, mentally or spiritually strong enough to face the issue, we may lower our guard and allow ourselves to see our pain. Have you experienced a sense of denial in your journey? Process any strong feelings that have erupted as you've lowered your guard and allowed the dreaded reality to rest on your mind.

As we processed the death of our child, we experienced the searing pain of disappointment, dread for the previously anticipated holidays, and waves of sadness that would wreck our sense of stability. Of course denial had felt safer in the moment.

As you take time to reflect, consider if you feel unsafe looking at your hurt. Pain avoidance is among the most common reasons to deny reality. But unfortunately, denying reality doesn't keep it from being real. However, denial does prevent us from being able to fully live. Many people around you are living in survival mode to cope, denying painful truths and trying to prevent them from rising to the surface.

Kay spent years denying the pain she'd suffered trying to survive. When her mother, June, took pills, she became a different person. One time Kay had to dig pills out of her mother's mouth, and once nearly had her finger bitten off as her mother attempted to take her own life in a drugged state. Kay remembers her mother moving them to Maine, Colorado, Alaska, and Hawaii in search of happiness. Each move pushed Kay further into survival mode.

One night, after years of sobriety, June casually referenced a desire to self-medicate with pills. Like a busted dam, Kay's mind was flooded with memories. She remembered when her mother had tried to make moves on her friends, yelled at her, and threw furniture and books across the room. June knew Kay loved books and found them comforting, a form of escape. Kay told her mom about her memories, one by one.

White, nearly frozen from the icy blast, June sat in shame as she listened. She easily could have denied she'd done these horrible things since she'd often blacked out and truly couldn't remember them. Instead, she asked, "How do you *not hate* me?" This question began to soften Kay's heart. The pain didn't vanish. But hearing her mom apologize and admit that these actions were part of her past broke through some of the walls of denial.

Kay grieved her childhood. She grieved that her mom didn't remember the ways she'd hurt her. She grieved that she felt a need to deny looking at these experiences for most of her life in order to survive. When we go through trauma or grief, it doesn't necessarily just go away with time. We can heal. But if we deny, we simply bury the pain and hope there is never enough rain to bring it back to the surface. Thankfully, when Kay was triggered, she tried to share how she felt from a positive space, and her mother responded relatively well. But we may still find ourselves coping in interesting ways, guarding against the possibility of experiencing negative emotions.

Grief is powerful. Grief can rob us. But it can also fill us with gratitude. When we heal, we can give others a blessing that results from our healing.

Take some time to ask yourself if you may be denying anything. Are there hurts that are too painful to acknowledge? The memories may not come to mind immediately, so be prepared for them to surface over the next few hours, days, or weeks.

Repression

Repression occurs when we deny an experience for so long that we are unable to remember it; typically, this is a subconscious process common for individuals who face trauma. One way we protect ourselves is by ignoring or suppressing any thoughts about the event. In one sense, this behavior can be healthy in the short term. We may need to tend to other tasks, so allowing ourselves to place our hurt on a "shelf" can be useful. But if we continue to stuff down our painful memories, we may become unable to access important information.

There is no magic tool to reveal repressed memories; however, creating a safe environment for community and connection often helps individuals access difficult, suppressed, and even some repressed memories.

Displacement

Have you ever been really mad about something that happened at work but found yourself taking it out on a family member or a pet? If so, then you have experienced displacement. When we intentionally or accidentally unleash frustration onto a safer or less powerful target, we displace our aggression. Sometimes we're mightily aware of this behavior, but other times we don't even see that we're avoiding an unmet need. Either way, our outbursts are an indicator that we're not okay.

Think about a time when you were hurting and someone needed your attention. It felt rude, disrespectful, maybe even impossible to handle. But they had no idea, and you didn't reveal your pain. You trudged on because that's what people do; you tried to listen as best you could. But then you got in your car, pulled up behind a slow driver, and felt an overpowering amount of rage shoot through your body and into the horn. For a moment, you almost felt better. Perhaps you just needed to let off a little steam.

> Displacement: releasing emotion onto a safer, typically less powerful target rather than the originating stimulus.

But it didn't really help. A little bit of guilt settled in. But the dialogue in your mind intensified: *get out of the way*. In those moments, consider asking this question: "Could there be anything else I'm angry about?" If you notice yourself expressing large amounts of anger when you usually don't, let that strike curiosity in you. Explore why the situation stirs up such strong feelings.

There are often other feelings behind our anger. Let's look at a work example. If we feel angry at our boss, what's behind our anger? Possibly we feel unseen and uncared for in our loss; it may be difficult to address the issue with a supervisor because we don't want to seem weak. Addressing it may make us feel vulnerable and set us up to feel lonely and rejected. These feelings can cause us to avoid addressing the issue. But if we resist expressing our emotions, we may explode or displace them onto a safer target. Will this help? Nope. It will tear down another relationship, likely one we need most right now.

So how do we avoid displacing our aggression? First, learn to note *when* you are displacing your aggression or other strong feelings onto a safer object. Once you become aware of what you have been doing, then you can look beneath the surface to identify the *why* behind your behavior.

Also ask yourself, "Why don't I feel safe to address my feelings with this individual? What am I afraid of?"

How many times do you think you have been the subject of someone else's displacement? We may take it personally if we don't recognize the behavior. The next time someone rages at you while driving, before becoming super upset, ask the question, "What if it's not personal?" Is it possible that the person is angry about something completely unrelated to your driving? Likely. Questions like these can bring so much freedom and enable us to release some of the emotions we stumble on in any given day.

If you find yourself frequently displacing strong emotions, consider ways you can practice being assertive. For example, if it's difficult for you to tell your boss when you're upset and you take it out on your family, spend time stretching yourself in unrelated areas. Ask a neighbor or coworker deeper questions or say hello to someone new. Stop by someone's office and ask, "How was your weekend?" When we practice assertions when it's unrelated to conflict or other strong feelings, it will build skills that can help when we face negative situations.

Rationalization

When we think of rationalization, the word that enters our minds is *excuses*. When our behavior doesn't line up with our beliefs, we may experience dissonance and therefore rationalize our behavior, excusing the actions that contradict our beliefs. Why?

At our core, we want to be *good*.

When we fail to meet that standard, we make excuses. We blame others. We do whatever it takes to protect ourselves from the painful reality that we are not as good as we would like to be.

Those of us who are parents aren't as good of parents as we told ourselves we would be when we judged others. And likely, we're not as good of employees, siblings, or friends as we sometimes think we are.

At work, once we got the position we'd coveted, we couldn't do all the things we said we would do when we complained to our coworkers about the last guy in that position. Why? We simply are not great at estimating how we will feel or act in the future. Remember, we're poor predictors of our future emotions. There are simply too many variables in life, and we are complex beings.

What's the lesson here? Let's expect that we will sometimes overestimate or underestimate our ability to be successful, to communicate well, or to bounce back after a loss. We can learn to recognize that we are making excuses, and we can ask people to call us out when they hear us rationalizing.

When was the last time you rationalized your behavior? Perhaps you thought, *I'll exercise tomorrow. I'll catch up on sleep this weekend. I'll do _____ later*. Examine your internal dialogue. Are you realistic or full of excuses? One of our favorite terms helps explain how we think differently when we make poor choices. *Fundamental attribution error* is a somewhat complicated social psychology term that can help explain why individuals struggle to get on the same page during conflict.[2] When we fail to return a phone call or text, we give a behavioral reason—an excuse for our lack of action. Yet when someone else ghosts us, we tend to attack their character, believing they are irresponsible or uncaring. Fundamental attribution error is a mental error that occurs when observing behaviors of oneself compared to the behavior of others. Personal behaviors are attributed to situational causes, while the behaviors of others are attributed to dispositional causes.

Do you see how complicated we are? We engage in mental gymnastics to protect our views of ourselves. Friends, we need Jesus! If we find ourselves making this error, let's commit to inviting God into the situation to help us empathize with the other person and behave in a God-honoring manner.

God's Word says, "Be transformed by the renewing of your mind" (Rom. 12:2 NIV). We're wired to protect ourselves, and because sin entered the world, we may deny, rationalize, or repress the truth. Jesus says in John 8:32 that "the truth will set you free." Invite God to renew your mind, grounding you and enabling you to see the truth even if it's painful. With God's help, you can let down your guard. Jesus's arms are strong. Feel His arms around you, saying, "My grace is sufficient for you, for my power is made perfect in weakness" (2 Cor. 12:9 NIV). God doesn't expect us to be strong; He knows we are dust (Ps. 103:14). He desires that we lean into Him because He is our strength and shield (Ps. 28:7).

God,
　　Please help me renew my mind so I can be free to fully grieve, love, and move forward. I'm leaning into Your grace today.

Amen.

seeing my world

Consider how your world has changed. As we step out into this new world, we may find we need additional skills to function. It may feel easier to avoid going places such as social gatherings, work, or church to preserve our emotional energy. When so much of our world changes, we feel less stable. But as we explore how our world has changed, we can gain skills to rebuild stability.

8 navigating my world

THE WORLD AROUND US looks different now. It may not feel as safe as it used to. Our normal routine has been interrupted, riddled with triggers, land mines that could be tripped at any moment. When we pass a coworker's office and hear them laugh, it could be another land mine. We wonder if we will ever be happy again. When a neighbor waves as they drive past our home, land mine. No one knows how we feel.

It's all right to be upset about the changes. Take a moment to identify these changes that grief blasted on your world. Perhaps your daily routine at home or work feels completely different. Going to the gym, church, or other activities can be overwhelming. Take time to explore your world. What feels safe? What feels difficult?

Will it always feel this heavy? Probably not exactly. But you loved deeply, which is why you are hurting. So let's explore your hurt so you can get back to deeply loving those who still care for you.

How do you fill in the blank? My world feels _____.

Many times, from 2015 to 2017, our world felt unstable, unpredictable, different, less joyful, incomplete, broken, lonely, missing something, gray, flat, lacking creativity.

Our grief resides within us, so everywhere we go may look a bit different. Consider how your world feels different and how you've coped.

My Coping Impacts My World

In chapter 3, we developed a list of positive and negative coping mechanisms. Reflect on the list and ask yourself, "How have my negative coping mechanisms impacted the people in my world?"

Ginger was lonely, so she filled many evenings with negative coping mechanisms, including Netflix and drinking, choosing to escape rather than allow her natural alert system to func-

> "How have my negative coping mechanisms impacted the people in my world?"

tion the way God intended. She grew less productive at work and ended up feeling grumpy most days. Because she was unhappy, she often isolated, turning down invitations to be with family and friends. Do you see how her negative coping behavior led her toward more negative experiences? Her world was impacted by her grief. Ginger had moved into a negative space. Her negative coping mechanisms begot more negative coping. However, she had some choices to make. She could look at her grief, or she could continue defensively protecting herself.

Ginger had unmet needs. She wanted to feel needed and to experience community, but her loneliness got in the way. When she took time to examine her needs, she could see the behaviors that were attempts to meet those needs. It is important to go a step further and look deeper. Ginger was lonely, but she was also afraid of rejection. She wanted to love again, but she had lost. She had been hurt. So she was tempted to isolate. But there was function in the dysfunctional behavior. Consider how Ginger's dysfunctional behavior helped her. The escape she experienced by drinking and immersing herself in entertainment allowed her to feel good momentarily. Additionally, the goal of isolation was to ward off future pain in the form of rejection. In the short term, she moved herself to a positive space; however, the negative coping mechanisms set her up to be in a negative space in the future. As Ginger looked at her unmet needs, her coping mechanisms, and the ways she tried to meet those needs in healthy and unhealthy ways, it became easier to see more beneficial alternatives. This enabled her to focus on long-term solutions that would meet her needs and help her build her house in a positive space.

Consider the impact that each of your positive and negative coping mechanisms has on your world. We cannot completely control our world, but we can change our behavior. It's amazing how much our behavior positively or negatively affects everything around us, especially our perception of the world.

We cannot completely control our world, but we can change our behavior.

Looking at My World

When you think about your world, how did you hope it would be different? Consider any unmet expectations you are living with.

Really, if we are honest, we may get a bit angry if we plan something and it doesn't turn out how we'd hoped. Consider a lighthearted example. If we choose to go on a vacation and it doesn't turn out great, we get upset. If the weather is bad or our kids misbehave, we tend to feel sorry for ourselves. We looked forward to this trip and saved money to make it happen, and it's a big disappointment. Don't we act similarly with our dreams and daily lives?

We watch movies with unrealistic, exceptionally happy endings. We save money for retirement and dream about what it will be like to travel the world. I, Ashley, am the worst at this regarding work. I work today so I can rest in the future. Nearly every day. The problem is, we are always living in *today*. If we do not find ways to enjoy today, we will eventually grow disappointed in the future.

Sometimes we have unrealistic expectations regarding the holidays too. For us, there were times when it felt unbearable to go through the holiday season; we were hoping to announce that we were expecting a baby. We went from being optimistic about the future to being filled with dread regarding events, entire days, or seasons.

When facing unmet expectations, we might feel tempted to stop dreaming. But dreaming is an amazing gift from God that we want to hold on to. But sometimes we dream and expect fairy tales to come true. Dreams are not reality. We live in a fallen world, and we will face hurdles, roadblocks, and pain along the way. How do we continue to dream, living with joy? If we take our unmet expectations to God and His Word, He holds the power to shift our focus, giving us contentment, joy, and the ability to see beauty amid sorrow.

Next, let's ask what we can do about our hurt. Take a moment to think about what might help. Here are a few ideas: journal, share your thoughts with a friend, pray, take a day off and spend it in nature or with family.

As we begin to explore why our world feels so different, reflect on any defense mechanisms you may be using. Our world can be difficult because our loved ones or our boss or others may not allow us to deny our pain. They may pry or ask questions we're not ready to face. If so, congratulations. You're seen. It's interesting how we can feel so bad about feeling unseen, yet when we are seen too much, we have problems with that too! We're so picky.

Or maybe your support system pushes you to deny your pain; they may be too busy with their own hurts or may not have the skills to help you. And that has allowed negativity to build. If your support system does not offer the grace you need, you may use defense mechanisms to meet your safety needs. Have you engaged in any defensive behavior that has negatively impacted your world? If so, identify what you have been trying to protect yourself from. Consider reading Ephesians 6:10–18 regarding the armor of God. God's armor protects us from our enemy, Satan, as well as our own defense mechanisms.

As we address our needs, we become empowered to meet them.

How My View of Work Has Changed

In what ways do you experience work differently? Maybe you find meetings difficult when you used to enjoy collaboration. Or perhaps coffeepot chatter has become especially burdensome. If you're finding it difficult to remember tasks or manage people well, you're not alone.

For our friend Cathy, work was an escape. It was the place she felt *almost* normal. Derek, however, could barely survive his weekly team meeting. Everyone came in laughing and making jokes, and then they jumped into complex statistics. Laughing felt impossible, almost as tough as processing data.

How My View of Family Has Changed

If your family has stepped up during your time of loss, perhaps you view them in a more positive light than previously. But oftentimes when we are grieving, we are disappointed with our family and wish they would reach out. We may compare their behavior with how we communicate our grief, tossing around mental accusations about why they aren't reacting in similar ways. This creates distance, especially when we remain silent, holding our thoughts in our mind's great abyss.

As you decide how to view your family, we encourage you to remember that they are likely doing the best they can. They may not be doing it right. It's okay to be disappointed, but don't let their choices define your character. Have you considered asking for what you want? This can make you feel vulnerable. But remember the Golden Rule (Matt. 7:12): treat others how you want to be treated. If the roles were reversed and you weren't meeting your family member's needs, wouldn't you want them to tell you? Often we wait so long to speak with our family about how we feel that we end up communicating from a negative space. Try to communicate with your family from a positive space. Perhaps you could simply start by sharing how your view of your family has shifted during this season.

How My View of the Church Has Changed

If the church is part of your world, then it is possible that your view of the church has changed since your loss. Has it changed for better or for worse? People in the church may have brought you comfort or pain, support or judgment, silence or too much direction.

Sometimes we feel unsupported by the church and decide God doesn't care. Frequently, humans dislike God because of their experiences with people. The church is a group of people. Unfortunately, it is possible that people may not care for us as much as we need or wish, but it is important to distinguish between the church and God. God instructs us to be the body of Christ (1 Cor. 12:26–27). He wants us to reach out and encourage others. However, we are imperfect people and can unintentionally (and sometimes intentionally) hurt others with our actions or inactions.

In what ways have you been encouraged by the church?

In what ways have you been discouraged by the church?

Have you blamed God for your disappointment in others?

Have you requested an appointment with a pastor or church leader to discuss your loss or your current needs?

If the church is part of our world, it is more likely that we will feel hurt by the people in it. If we hang out with people in a bar, we will be hurt by people in a bar. If we hang out with people in the church, we will be hurt by people in the church. It's a human problem. Let's determine to get to the other side of this so we can heal and be the body of Christ, offering the community to others that we wish we had experienced during our season of loss. We hope the church will remain a source of comfort and healing for you as you process the ways your world has changed.

> God,
>
> My world feels wrecked by grief. Sometimes I'm so overwhelmed that I don't know what to do. Help me run to You with the broken pieces of what used to be. You are my Redeemer. I acknowledge that You can redeem what has been lost.
>
> Amen.

9 unexpected new skills needed

WHEN WE FACE LOSS, we may find that we suddenly need skills we never learned. We unexpectedly wish we had become a lawyer, had the skill to write an obituary, or had pursued a different career so we could escape to the mountains and live off the land. When we feel mentally stable, we tend to be more comfortable learning new skills. But grief doesn't seem to care. "You feel weak and unstable?" Grief asks. "Oh well. Sink or swim."

If you didn't know how to swim before now, it may not feel like the ideal time to learn, but out of necessity, we hope you choose to swim. The needs that arise out of grief expose a use for new skills. We call these "grief needs." We don't recall anyone teaching us how to talk about our grief needs. Mostly, we see many people avoid talking about grief. But we believe you are resilient and can learn new skills even when you're struggling.

Let's look at a couple of examples from Scripture of individuals who suddenly needed some new skills. Esther learned that her people were going to be killed. She was torn because she would have to put her life on the line (Esther 4:10–5:3).

She didn't feel like she had the authority (or skill) to go before
the king. Esther surely faced dissonance and fear, yet she was
encouraged by her cousin Mordecai that it was possible that
she was made queen "for just such a time as this" (v. 14). What
about David (1 Sam. 16:11–13)? His father didn't think of him as
a suitable king, so much so that when Samuel came to select a
king, his father didn't call for him. He didn't appear to have
a kingly demeanor. David wasn't used to Saul's armor and
didn't feel comfortable using it; nothing seemed quite right.
Yet David stepped out in fear, surely battling a bit of uncertainty before advancing in faith. His faith in God plus his fear
of God outweighed his fear of inadequacy.

What new skills do you need? Take action.
Find someone to connect with, perhaps a
modern-day Mordecai. As you seek community, we pray you will find strength. Do it in

> Do it in fear.
> Do it in faith.

fear. Do it in faith. Do it in fear of God. Do it even if you feel
fearful. Do it in faith that God is bigger than any of your fears!

Perhaps your inner dialogue raged as you read the last paragraph. If you said, "My new title is not king or queen as it was
for David or Esther. My new title is unemployed, widower, or
barren. What good can come from these titles?" First, we are
so sorry for your unwanted title. But we're so glad you asked
what good can come from it. We wonder how David felt as he
kept the sheep that day when Samuel came to anoint one of
his brothers as king. Do you think he knew Samuel was coming and he wasn't seen as an option? It's possible his brothers
acted awkwardly in the moments leading up to the event because they didn't want David to know. David had opportunities
to feel bad about himself or his family. Yet, miraculously, he
believed in himself. More so, he believed in God's power to
work through him.

Do you believe this same power lives in you? You can live *stuck*, focusing on the painful new titles and unexpected skills that are needed, or you can live a life propelled by faith in God, as David and Esther did. But this process takes time. If you commit to daily community with God, He will transform your beliefs about yourself and help you see that He is able to help you heal, using your pain for His glory.

We encourage you to invite God to help you process the new skills that are needed for the unwanted title you've received. Ask God to help you see how He can transform you (Rom. 12:2) so that He will receive glory from the tragedies you've faced. After all, no one likes to see the bad guys win at the end of the story, eh?

Acquiring New Skills

When our world was shut down by the pandemic, many people had to learn how to use Zoom and other forms of technology. We quickly needed new skills to survive. A good friend of ours lost her husband very suddenly. He had taken great care of her by tending to many things in the home. This was a blessing to her but left her overwhelmed in his absence. Sometimes the biggest blessings can become our greatest trials. Likely, you had no way of knowing you would need these skills. Or if you did, perhaps you were busy or in denial. Regardless, we cannot go back. We can simply determine if we will learn the new skill or if we will find another way to meet the need.

When I, Ashley, lost my job, we also lost financial security. We needed money-making and money-saving skills. Thankfully, I had lived on very little as I paid my way through college, so this skill was solid. But I needed money-making skills. I connected with others and worked several part-time jobs until securing something full-time.

When we lost our first child, we quickly became concerned. My mom had lost four babies, so we began asking questions and looking for correlations. After our second loss, I became a researcher, spending hour after hour scouring research journals on recurrent miscarriage. We scheduled an appointment to meet with a specialist during our pregnancy, and then, a couple of days before the appointment, we lost the baby. We went to the appointment anyhow because we hoped the doctor would provide some options. The doctor ran tests on our baby and offered his insight on how to proceed in the future. We decided to try a treatment that my mom had found successful after her losses. Our situations required unexpected new skills. So we learned.

When we lost our next baby, even while using the specialist-recommended treatment, we decided to see a couple of other specialists. Unfortunately, the available research for our situation was minimal; oftentimes cases like ours were identified as outliers and eliminated from studies. But we read between the lines. We compared studies and saw potential. We discussed options with our specialist, and he agreed to a treatment option we suggested. Surprisingly, he said that years prior, he had used one of the treatments we discovered and had found it effective for rare cases such as ours.

We share this story because we're aware that you may also feel deficient. You can never learn enough to avoid the pain of loss. But it may be possible for you to read and digest heavy academic material enough to ask questions of a specialist. Or it may be possible to learn whatever skill that feels insurmountable to you. We were overwhelmed by the new skills we were lacking, but we pushed anyhow. We chose to get to work and are so thankful we did. Our son is a constant reminder of how the combination of faith, resilience, research, and prayer can yield beautiful, miraculous works.

Spiritual Skills Needed

We need God now more than ever. Actually, that's not true. We've always needed Him more than we need air. With each passing moment, we need Him. It's time to *do* the things we know to do. We need to engage in God's Word, absorbing His guidance daily. If you're already reading the Bible regularly, talk with someone about what you're reading. If you've gained comfort talking with someone about what you're reading, consider engaging someone new regarding God's Word. Join a group, build the discipline of deepening your faith. Remember that faith comes by hearing and hearing by the Word of God (Rom. 10:17).

> It's time to *do* the things we know to do.

When Cho lost his wife, he took only a few days off work. Then when he exploded on a coworker (remember that term *displacement?*), the individual lovingly offered to accompany him to a grief group held at a nearby church. Cho didn't realize that was exactly what he needed. He needed God. He needed to be seen. He wanted to get control of the areas of his life that he felt had fallen far out of his control. The group helped him renew hope, and later, he decided to become a facilitator. Cho learned a new skill so he could help himself, and as a result, he has also helped hundreds of others restore their lives.

Communication Skills Needed

Have you ever felt completely unsure how to respond to unfiltered or "spiritual" comments people make regarding your loss? Perhaps someone has told you, "God's got this," "They're in a better place," or "God must have needed an angel." These comments are like spiritual bandages, but the only one who feels better is the person who says the comment. The individual may feel more spiritual for pointing the person to God, but the griever is often left feeling guilty or unspiritual, questioning what's wrong with them for feeling sad or not having enough faith. We need strong communication skills to prevent relational breakdown in these situations. This is an example of a need that may become more evident with loss.

I, Ashley, withdrew from investing in others because some "Christian" remarks (or silence) felt overwhelming. This was a negative coping mechanism I used to protect myself. Withdrawing was dysfunctional, but what was the function? The function was self-protection, but in the process, I quickly found myself feeling alone (hello, dysfunction!).

Do you ever feel like words are hard? Sometimes it's easier to keep them inside. Think of a time when you withheld your feelings from someone. There was a reason you kept your words locked inside. It's appropriate at times to keep our thoughts to ourselves, pray through them, or send them directly to God, asking Him to purify our minds. But when we face difficulties and don't want to displace our aggression, the best remedy is to communicate. Ask someone to spend time with you. Tell someone you need them. See a coach or counselor. They'll help you build communication skills.

As we faced the loss of our children, I, Chuck, learned that guys often struggle to communicate with their wives, especially regarding difficult topics such as loss. I've met numerous guys who have shared that they experienced loss in ways that were vastly different from their wives. These men worried that if they didn't hurt the same way as their wives, they were doing it wrong and shouldn't share. With our losses, I felt like a failure because I was unable to protect our child. There was nothing I could do, and as a provider and protector of the family, I felt helpless. As I shared these thoughts with other men, they related.

82 | seeing my world

If we do not talk about our feelings, others cannot relate to us. When we communicate, we can overcome.

Reflect on how you learned to communicate. Perhaps the names of people who lived in your home popped into your head. Especially if you lived with a poor communicator, give yourself time to rewire your automatic thinking and communication patterns. It's important that we strengthen our connection to God, improve our communication skills, and develop a healthy support system so we can build stability that will secure *us* and others for the future.

Learning new skills is challenging on a good day. Learning new grief skills is taxing but can also be exhilarating because we are resilient. We do hard things. We bring God into our negative spaces.

God,

You know my present and future needs before I even bring them to You. Give me patience with myself and others as I develop these skills. I look to You because You're my Teacher.

Amen.

10 avoiding painful triggers

CONSIDER WHAT TRIGGERS YOU regarding your loss. There may be specific places you have found extra troubling to visit. Whether a hospital, restaurant, or grocery store, strong feelings are associated with our personal triggers. Because certain places trigger a strong emotional reaction within you, it feels safer to avoid them. We'll share some stories about our triggers and what we learned. Along the way, we will discuss terms and ideas to consider as you process your loss.

When I lost my job and Chuck failed out of his first semester of college, we both had strong reactions. I wanted to avoid talking about or visiting locations near that establishment for a while, and Chuck wanted to avoid his former college's campus. Wow. As we step back and read that, we hope you can find encouragement. If God can use us, people who have lost a job and failed a semester of college, what can God do with your situation? We encourage you to seek God as you explore the places you've avoided as a result of your loss. Where are these places? Consider what needs have been met through avoidance.

Immediately after each of our miscarriages, we found it excruciating to drive past the hospital where our babies would have been born. And this was a difficult task to avoid, considering we can see the hospital when we look out our bedroom window. When we were "expecting," we began to change our *expectations* of life. We anticipated meeting our baby and adding a member to our family; therefore, we began preparing our home. These hopes led to behavioral changes that would later become triggers. Seeing the hospital previously triggered hopeful emotions. After our loss, the same building paired with our unmet expectations triggered grief, sadness, and disappointment. In your life, what triggers are you facing? Consider if these triggers previously stimulated joy or if they always brought feelings of sadness.

When it felt overwhelming to drive past the hospital, we gave ourselves permission to travel a different route. This helped when our loss was fresh. In time, we worked to neutralize our triggers through a process called *reframing*. We knew it wasn't healthy to avoid the hospital indefinitely, so we talked about it with each other. We shared how we felt disappointed but were thankful we had a hospital we could go to when we felt unwell. This was reinforced when one of us needed to visit urgent care. We were so thankful we could get medical attention and have worked to remind ourselves that although the hospital had been a source of loss and pain, it also brings healing and restoration.

> We worked to neutralize our triggers through a process called *reframing*.

I, Chuck, enjoy jogging and found it difficult to run around the hospital for several weeks after our losses. Early one morning, I felt it would be good for me to "go there" physically and emotionally. As I approached one building, I began thinking about our losses and what life could have been. I used to be expecting a little one to join our family. And then everything changed.

As I started the loop around the hospital campus, warm tears began to well up in my eyes. With each step, the wind chased the tears down the sides of my face. Emotions surged. I began to sob. The intensity grew until I needed to stop running. As I walked, I "went there." To this day, it's one of most emotional experiences I've encountered. It was also empowering. It didn't kill me, but it hurt to allow the feelings into the present moment. Before I completed the loop around the hospital, I experienced anger, sadness, relief, God's comfort, and clarity. When I began to run again, I felt better—a little lighter. I think it was more than the calorie loss from the intense jogging session! I felt more connected to the baby we lost. I had been avoiding the very feelings I needed to experience in order to gain a sense of freedom. Perhaps you, too, have been avoiding some feelings you need to face; freedom may lie on the other side.

We can easily displace our emotions. Hospitals have been established around the world to provide expert medical care to individuals in need. Daily, lives are saved in hospitals. Yet, for us, the hospital triggered pain. In reality, it wasn't the enemy. In fact, this hospital in particular has been a part of some of the best days of our lives; it's where we met our living sons for the first time. Once I processed my grief during the run, I could release some of the pain and lean into gratitude. It wasn't easy, but I feel less scared to "go there" now.

Another benefit of us facing our emotions has been that we're able to let go of some of the hurt, allowing us to visit the

Reframe: to change the way one thinks or behaves regarding a matter.

hospital without being paralyzed by our emotions. We can see individuals from church who are staying there for care without being overwhelmed by our own past sorrow. It's our hope that you find strength and perspective as you move through each day. May whatever it is that brought you to this book become a source of resilience in your life, resulting in healing for you and inspiration for others.

Avoidant Behavior

What places have you avoided? Process which emotions are triggered when you visit these locations. We offer you permission to take care of yourself. Give yourself space to travel a slightly different route home if it helps you feel a little bit better. But more importantly, we want to help you understand the true motivation behind your behavior. Take time to understand why avoiding feels safer. As you understand yourself better, we hope you'll be able to meet your need. Then avoidance will no longer be needed.

When my (Ashley) grandfather was alive, he and my mom loved visiting a local burger and shake shack and watching movies at a nearby theater. After he passed, we didn't go to the movies or that restaurant for a while. One day, we missed Grandpa and decided to visit that restaurant. Interestingly, we were served by a lady who had also waited on Grandpa many times. This added to the experience and helped us feel connected to him. It was okay to avoid the restaurant for a while, but when we finally visited this place he loved, we felt closer to him. Think about the places you've avoided. Will there be a time when you'll feel comfortable visiting this place again? Consider the needs that are being met by avoiding this place. As you explore these needs, you can work toward meeting them in healthier ways.

Emotional Avoidance

Maybe the "places" you've avoided aren't physical; perhaps they're emotional. You may find yourself controlling conversations to keep your emotions locked in a vault and avoid discussing deep, meaningful topics. You may also control conversations because it's overwhelming to carry someone else's pain when you're struggling. You may not feel as empathetic as usual, causing you to withdraw emotionally. When we avoid, there's always a reason. Take some time to reflect on the "good" you see in the behavior. What's good about withdrawing? Let's pause and take this to God. Ask Him to help you see what good has come from your avoidant behavior so you can meet your needs in healthier ways.

If you're withdrawing from healthy relationships, there's a positive reason you're doing so, but more harm than good comes from long-term withdrawal. First, let's explore the good. Then we'll dive into the not so good. Usually we're trying to protect ourselves from something, and that can be very important. God created us to care for ourselves. With some of our losses, we withdrew emotionally, keeping our pain to ourselves because of the hurtful comments some people made.

Another function that comes from keeping our emotions locked away is that when we avoid, we can sort of pretend we feel normal. Again, let's explore the function in the dysfunction. It's good that we want to be okay. And it's good that we value stability. But it's not good if we lock away our emotions, trying to fool ourselves into believing we're okay when we're really suffering.

After we see the function in the dysfunction, we can aim to meet the need in a healthier way. Although withdrawal meets some of our needs, let's be sure to examine whether it leads to a fuller life. It may be good to rest or protect, but withdrawal can also create distance in relationships that may lead to loneliness.

As you continue to explore if you have a pattern of withdrawal, consider if you've ever avoided church.

Avoiding Church

What if the place you've wanted to avoid is church? Eek. Hopefully that isn't you, but if it is, we can relate.

There were times we were overwhelmed with grief and felt anxious going to church or church-related events. Days after I discovered Chuck had been looking at pornography, we were supposed to attend a ministry retreat together. Chuck felt ashamed and distant from God and Ashley, yet he knew he needed to draw closer, not further, from us. I cried much of the drive to the retreat. My dreams of doing ministry together felt shattered, and I didn't know how I should act. Though we felt uncertain, in the end, we were both thankful we went. We grew spiritually and learned to work through our emotions in a spiritual setting.

Zip along to 2016 when we lost our second baby to miscarriage. When we walked into church, I was greeted by a sweet friend who said, "Hey, mama! How are you?" Though this comment triggered great sorrow, I remained calm. After all, I could tell she felt terrible for hurting me. But as we turned the corner to walk down the hall, I wished I could duck into a room, climb out the window, and return to the safety of our home. But I didn't. I continued, and I spoke to others. I dropped off our kiddos for class and cried throughout worship.

So although we permitted ourselves to travel a different route to avoid passing the hospital, we didn't allow ourselves to stay home from church. We knew it was too important. God is important, and He's our only source of true healing. We were still ministry leaders who continued to pour into others through worship leadership, teaching, and discipleship. But remember earlier how we mentioned that we withdrew? When we found that we didn't want to withdraw physically, we coped by withdrawing emotionally from time to time. Looking back, we wish we would have reached out to more people to share how we were hurting. But we didn't always feel comforted by the common grief responses offered. Instead, we shared with only a few individuals. What's behind your need to withdraw or avoid places, people, or things?

Moving Away from Avoidance

We may want to avoid going into a restaurant or church or even a room in our home. But it's okay to go to some places we dread. It may even be good for us. Because if we don't go, we can reinforce negative tendencies. Here are a few questions to help you decide if you should go back to places that trigger pain:

1. Do you have positive memories or the possibility of forming future positive memories there?
2. Will you be able to avoid this place forever? If not, when might you be forced (or need) to visit? What kind of day will that be, triggering strong emotions? Would it be better to take control now so you don't feel out of control on that unpredictable day?
3. What problems have resulted from your avoidance? For example, has it cost you extra time and money?
4. What are the benefits to going back? Could it bring freedom?

Consider another example. At a memorial service, have the smells, sounds, and other experiences thrown you into the past? Entering the building may have triggered a past memory or even a traumatic event. I, Ashley, found myself needing to comfort others at my grandfather's funeral. As visitors hugged my mom and me, they shared how difficult the experience was for *them*. One said, "The last time I was at a funeral home was for my father." Another comment was, "It's amazing. It's been fifteen years since I lost my mom. It never really gets easier."

These individuals meant well when they came to support my mom. However, their unprocessed grief spilled over, making it difficult to properly support her. If we determine to work through our grief, we will be more capable of helping others down the road.

When we understand our triggers, we can neutralize them by increasing our awareness of our strong emotions. This gives us permission to grieve, even if that means breaking down in the middle of a run.

We're unaware of any Scriptures that instruct us to *avoid* bringing our hurts to God. If we want to bring them to God, spending our time avoiding them will make it unlikely that we will share them with Him or others. God invites us to come to Him when we are weary, and He will give us rest (Matt. 11:28). Rather than avoid looking at our pain, let's run to God.

God,

I'm here. You ask me to come to You when I am weary. I'm weary. Show me the things I've avoided. Help me sort through the whys behind my behavior. I need You. I need You. I need You.

Amen.

11   how I look at changes around me

AS YOU REFLECT on your defense mechanisms, unmet needs, new skills needed, and places you've avoided, think of what you've learned about yourself. If you've defensively protected yourself by avoiding places and engaging in other protective behaviors, it's possible you're living in a negative space. If so, you could be looking at the world through a foggy lens. When we look at the hospital and feel like we hate it, we've got a foggy lens. Imagine you just purchased new prescription lenses. If the lenses were foggy, it would impact how you saw the entire world. When we have dirty lenses, why don't we just clean them, already?

It's not always that easy. Remember the Three A's to Change. The first step is to become *aware*. Sometimes we aren't even aware that we have a skewed view of the world. Or we may know our lens has become cloudy, but we do not believe we have what it takes to clean it. Since the first step is to become aware, set a goal to increase your consciousness about the lens through which you view the world. This takes a bit of focus. Invite God to help you see if you have a foggy lens, then sit and process.

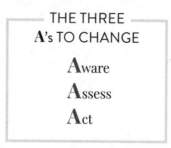

> ### THE THREE
> ### A's TO CHANGE
>
> **A**ware
>
> **A**ssess
>
> **A**ct

When our view of the world is skewed, we tend to feel a bit skeptical, expecting people to hurt or leave us. But simply removing a skeptical lens is not always so easy.

The second A is to *assess*. During the assessment process, we can ask deep, meaningful questions about ourselves and others. What has worked? What hasn't? What have we tried? What could we try? Unless we look at the good in the negative behavior, we cannot fully understand how we need to change.

So let's explore what works about skepticism. Skepticism protects us by keeping us from experiencing the disappointment that results from unmet expectations. But without hopeful expectations about life, we tend to drift toward loneliness, anxiety, or depression. Be sure to look deeply at the pain that has also come from skepticism. When you contemplate everything you've tried to help meet your needs, consider if you were in a negative or positive space. Many times we think our efforts to meet our needs failed, but in reality, they didn't work because they were made in a negative space.

Consider Ethan's difficult situation. His spouse left him. He's in a negative space and sees people differently. When his lens was clear, he could welcome others' efforts to connect. But with a cloudy lens, he perceives a friend's outreach as something to avoid. After facing rejection and judgment, he began to fear that his friends might say they want to hang out, when in reality, they only want something from him. There may be some good that comes from your behavior (that's the *function* in the dysfunction), but be sure to explore the dysfunction too.

Now, look at what you've tried in the past and what you can try in the future. Make a list. As you consider options, think outside the box. So often people believe they have "tried everything" when they've tried only a few options, and some of them were done from a negative space. Instead of saying no to every invitation, you could say yes to all. You could say yes about half the time, or you could say yes to one out of every three invitations. You could also initiate instead of waiting to turn someone else down. You could write down quotes and phrases to help you fight skepticism. Do you see that our options are truly endless? Have you ever felt like facing your emotions could overtake you? The good news is that our emotions can also empower us. Our actions seem to be the determining factor in whether we feel empowered or defeated by our emotions.

The third A is to *act*. How will Ethan act now that he's aware of his thoughts and actions and has assessed the why behind his behavior? Ethan could *deny* that his view of the world has shifted, that he has a foggy lens. And he would stay stuck. Or he could explore how his lens became cloudy. If he looks at how he sees the world, he can open himself up to heal. In the action stage, we can review the menu of options we developed in the assessment process and then make a move. Then we can continue working through the Three A's to Change again and again.

Consider Jenna, who kept cleaning her lenses. Her husband, Preston, spoiled her nearly every day of their thirty-six-year marriage. When he died suddenly, she had never pumped gas. In the first two weeks after her husband passed, her son filled up her tank so she wouldn't have to. But Jenna was determined to do it on her own. As she nervously stepped out of her car and carefully read the screen on the pump, deciding whether she wanted a car wash, premium gas, or a receipt, her eyes welled up with tears. And then she laughed. "Honey, if you were here, you would have jumped out of the car to fill up the tank. You spoiled me, but I can do this. Nope, I don't want a car wash. No, I don't want a receipt. And nah, I don't want premium gas."

Jenna was in a positive space with her husband when he passed, so although this experience triggered strong emotions for her, she also felt connected to him, remembering the love he had for her. She didn't want to forget that. When negative thoughts crept in, she redirected her thinking to the reason her husband had pumped her gas in the first place. He loved her!

Do you think Jenna's choice to laugh and look at the good memories of her husband helped her hold on to the love she had for him? Or would it have been better for her to live in a negative space? So often, people feel guilty for being joyful, as if it's harmful or insulting to their loved ones who are gone. But this is a distorted reality. When we pass away, don't we want our loved ones to think about us? And we don't want to bring more hurt than they've already experienced from losing us. We want them to laugh and embrace the memories we shared together rather than bury them forever. If we want these good things for our loved ones, we can assume they would want the same for us.

Moving Back to a Positive Space

Do you relate to Jenna or Ethan, being in a positive or a negative space, having a clear or foggy lens? Either way could be a sign of profound love being overshadowed by deep grief. Whatever negative habits you've started can be unlearned. We have authority over our thoughts. Although we may not be able to directly prevent some thoughts from entering our mind, we may choose to stop thinking of intrusive ones, redirecting ourselves to different, positive thoughts. In 2 Corinthians 10:5, we are challenged to "take captive every thought to make it obedient to Christ" (NIV).

We can stop our negative thoughts and replace them with more accurate statements. This is how we clean our lens. For example, if the following enters your mind—"I can't do this anymore"—recognize it as a negative thought. It is an indication that you've moved into a negative space. This is step 1, being aware of your thoughts and behavior. Then, assess. You've recognized the negative thought. Now, be more specific. Be curious, asking yourself, "What is overwhelming me right now?" By stopping the negative thought and being curious about the emotion you're experiencing in the present, you free yourself up to tackle one situation rather than your entire life at once. Let's say you would answer the question "What is overwhelming me right now?" by saying, "I feel unequipped to handle stress." You can assess options and move toward action. As you look directly at the changes that prompted the negative emotions, you can more easily make a decision that will help you feel supported. You're part of your own support system. Support yourself by being aware of how you look at the changes around you. After you've noted that you feel overwhelmed by stress, you can replace the thought with another. Act by saying, "This is what grit looks like. I am pressing on even when it feels difficult."

Escaping Negative Spaces

While Jenna seemed to use a healthy approach, let's look at Ty's situation. Ty lived in a negative space. His wife, Savannah, an officer in the Air Force, was recently promoted and they moved to Eielson, Alaska, which was seventeen hours away from their families. Ty struggled to find a job he felt proud of and frequently complained to the new people he met. When his wife shared exciting moments from her day, he felt resentful. Ty was in a negative space and depressed.

Let's discuss how we used the Three A's to Change to help Ty understand what was going on inside him. The first step is to become *aware*. By asking, "What is overwhelming you right now?" we helped Ty bring his feelings into conscious awareness. Ty answered, "I feel stuck, wishing we had not moved." Ty had agreed to move, but he'd thought it would be easier to find a job he loved. When we dug a little deeper, Ty shared that he felt distant from Savannah and jealous that she was so happy when he wanted to leave.

As we listened and moved to the second A (*assess*), we learned that Ty had not shared his feelings with his wife. He didn't want to burst her bubble. With the assessment process, we wanted to consider all the options Ty had tried and some he could attempt in the future, so we challenged him to brainstorm options. He shared that he'd tried very few solutions in the past but that moving forward he could speak with Savannah, run away (we encouraged him to think of some *wild* options also), join a gym, attend a men's Bible study at church, or speak with people at church regarding local job opportunities. Some of these options would directly meet his needs while others may not. It was helpful to explore how to directly meet his identified unmet need. He felt unseen and realized that his silence and isolation had contributed to feelings of depression.

Ty was in a negative space while his wife was in a positive space, loving her new job. She felt love and great appreciation for his willingness to move across the country so she could pursue her dreams. Since Ty had not told her that he was upset, she didn't know that help was needed. Savannah had asked him a couple of times if everything was okay because he seemed a little quiet. But when he assured her that he was fine, she dismissed those signals.

PERCEIVED RELATIONSHIP

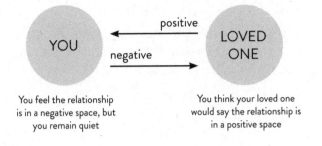

You feel the relationship
is in a negative space, but
you remain quiet

You think your loved one
would say the relationship is
in a positive space

Ty continued to drift apart from Savannah. He became quieter, feeling as if they were growing apart. This behavior is all too common. In fact, one of the top reported reasons for divorce is that the couple *grew apart*.[1] Ty realized he needed to share his feelings with Savannah, which moved him to the third A—*act*. From there, they began working on solutions.

While Jenna seemed to look through a clear lens, for a season, Ty saw the world through a foggy lens. But he learned to communicate even when it was difficult, and he was able to gain clarity and move closer to his wife. This enabled him to feel safe enough to meet people and build friendships.

Maybe you've experienced something similar. Have you sat quietly in a negative space, allowing a loved one to think you're in a positive space? Use the graphic above to assist you with the evaluation process. Be aware of your thoughts, feelings, and actions. Do you have a foggy lens? Assess what you've done that helps you feel seen. Explore efforts you've tried in the past and whether your tactics brought success. Then look for methods to try in the future. And lastly, act. Remember that your actions may not lead to perfect success, but you are working to create new habits. Invite God into your negative spaces, asking Him to shift your perspective where needed.

God,

   When my world feels distorted and foggy, give me Your eyes. Help me remember to take my thoughts captive and run to You for guidance.

                                                    Amen.

12 | work-grief balance

CONSIDER THE TERM *work-life balance*. Many people struggle with balancing their home and work lives. Similarly, we may engage in a struggle with our *work-grief balance*. Whether we're grieving a lost relationship, the loss of a pet, or a financial loss, grief over that situation impacts many areas of our life, including our work at home and the office. We cannot simply turn off our pain. Our defense mechanisms can trick us into thinking we're experts at compartmentalizing, but the effect loss has on our ability to work is immense. The intensity of the hurt combined with the reality that weakness is not rewarded in the workplace may tempt us to suppress our grief.

Employers are impacted by their employees' losses as well. The Grief Recovery Institute estimated that grief costs businesses $75 billion annually in lost or poor productivity, as well as lost business.[1] What if employees didn't feel the pressure to be so strong, to hide their losses, or to produce high-quality work the week they discovered their spouse is leaving them or they lost a baby to miscarriage or experienced the death of a beloved pet? Could that enable them to heal more quickly, feel seen, and get back to work?

Grief can interfere with our ability to think clearly or function as usual. Frequently, with the loss of a loved one comes

The Grief Recovery Institute estimated that grief costs businesses $75 billion annually in lost or poor productivity, as well as lost business.

new responsibilities, such as planning a memorial service, meeting with lawyers, or sorting through the deceased's belongings. This added pressure can cause tension that impacts others as well. At work, where weaknesses are frequently hidden, grieving may not feel welcomed or allowed.

Taking Grief to Work

I experienced my first miscarriage during the summer. I was teaching at a university, so I had a few weeks to recover before going back to work. Our second loss resulted in my passing the baby at home the night before returning to work for the semester. It was so difficult to sit through meetings and try to keep going, but I didn't want to stay home and sulk either. Knowing how to grieve appropriately can be difficult, especially if we don't have an example to follow or a policy to tell us it's okay to grieve.

A few months later, while in the middle of teaching a psychology course, I looked up as the classroom door opened. One of my coworkers motioned me to the hallway and told me our boss and her daughter (one of my students) had been killed in a car accident. *But I spoke with her yesterday*, I thought. I was calm but deeply saddened. I returned to the classroom, took a deep breath, and informed my students, dismissing class for the day. The next few days were very difficult as we continued to work, process, and grieve. I don't remember any coworkers asking how I was. My boss knew me better than anyone else at work. She encouraged me. She was an advocate when systems needed to be established or repaired. And she was gone. Suddenly.

I was pregnant again but hadn't told my boss yet. As I stood at the funeral, I discreetly placed a hand on my stomach, getting as close to holding our tiny one as possible. I grieved that I had not told my boss I was expecting, but I also knew how quickly my little one's heart could stop beating.

The next few days and weeks were a blur. The school didn't fill my boss's position, and there was little comfort or structure to help provide solace. We lost the baby, and I operated on autopilot. I taught classes and ducked into my office, doing my best to stay strong. I didn't feel like myself, so I didn't act like my typical, energetic self either, investing in students. Instead, I needed someone to ask about me.

Grief impacts nearly every aspect of our lives. Are you having a tough time at work? Is there someone you can speak with? It could be as simple as asking someone in human resources if there are any resources available for you. Or if you find yourself unable to meet a deadline, be honest with yourself and those you work with. Tell them you're having a tough time.

Give yourself permission to grieve, even at work. Over the years, there have been a few times when I have closed the door to my office and cried or gotten on my knees to seek God's help. In addition to bringing God into your negative space, here are some additional ideas to consider:

1. Be sure at least one person at work knows what's going on in your world.
2. Explore the areas where you're having the most difficult time because of your grief. For example, if creative tasks are more difficult, is it possible to delay or re-assign them for now?

3. Ask for what you need. Don't wait for someone to notice or take care of you.
4. Take care of yourself by getting enough sleep, food, exercise, and time with God.
5. Take control of your schedule as best as possible. Be intentional about when to say yes or no to meetings, invitations, etc.

After you've worked through your losses, become determined to see other people's grief. And if you can ensure that resources are available for others who face loss, do so. Many workplaces offer amazing support to those facing loss, and many of these resources were developed after people healed and decided to build a support system for others.

Give yourself permission to grieve, even at work.

How Should We Handle Grief?

It can be difficult to know how to respond to our heartbreak. Should we stay home? Should we push through and go to work? Or should we give ourselves permission to rest? Though it would be great for each of us to have an exact playbook to follow, life isn't that predictable. Sometimes we may think it's best to work and keep pushing through. And that's okay. But it's also fine if we get there and, realizing we're not okay, take a break, speak with someone about our feelings, and possibly even go home.

For us, we have memories of going to work when it probably would have helped our family if we had stayed home and processed our grief. But we didn't. Perhaps it was because no one told us we could. But it was also our own way of coping. We didn't want to sit and wallow; we didn't find that helpful. But we would have loved if our workplaces had offered resources to help us feel stronger during tough times.

Hungry

Angry

Lonely

Tired

When to HALT

We use the acrostic HALT to help us determine if we need to take a break or a personal day. Don't get too hungry, angry, lonely, or tired. This acrostic comes from the addictions field, but it's helpful in many other situations. If we're aware of our state of mind, we can learn to deescalate, calming our thoughts when we become too hungry, angry, lonely, or tired. Feeling unseen and less empathetic in any of these states, we may be triggered to move toward a negative space.

We could probably add a lot of other emotional experiences to that list. If we encounter strong emotions of fear, sadness, or being extremely hot or cold, it's important to be aware of them. Only then can we regulate and work through them. If we're at work and realize it's too difficult to sit through a meeting because we're grieving and emotionally tired, we should be honest with ourselves about how we feel. If tension is building, we should listen to our emotions and engage in self-regulation practices. For example, we could excuse ourselves and walk to the restroom to catch our breath. Or, in some situations, it could be helpful to share with colleagues what we're facing or respond in another way.

In fall 2017, we had an ultrasound scheduled for an early morning before work. At a previous appointment, we had found out that we were expecting and there were two gestational sacs. A nurse told us it looked like only one baby was healthy but nonchalantly said, "We will see at the next appointment." Looking back, we probably should've scheduled that appointment for the end of the day, but we didn't. And when we found out the second baby didn't make it, the nurse focused on the healthy baby. We were so thankful that one baby was growing inside my body, but we still grieved. I had about thirty minutes during my commute to process our loss, then it was back to work. Because it was warm, I moved class outside, thinking the sunshine might bring comfort. Although the topic for the day was not related to miscarriage, a student shared a story that cut my heart. He said he had a coworker who came to work after having a miscarriage, and he wondered why. He said, "I felt like the right thing for her to do was to go home and be with her family and grieve her loss." Punched in the stomach, I needed his words. Without ever knowing it, he gave me permission to go home. To hold myself together and not be too obvious since my students didn't know I was pregnant or that I just found out I used to be a mom of twins, I waited a few minutes and then dismissed class early.

We're not sure what would've happened if I would've stayed at work that day. Perhaps nothing major. And we don't exactly feel like it would have been best for me to stay home some of the other days that I chose to go into work. But we cannot always trust our initial emotions to lead us. We want to listen to the alerts our emotions offer and then assess our needs and how to meet them in the healthiest way possible, inviting God to guide us.

Grief Impacts Our Volunteer Work

I volunteer at church in different capacities, including leading worship. I've led on exciting and excruciating days. A few years ago, one of the songs on the set was "No Longer Slaves." On Wednesday evening, during rehearsal, as we sung the words "from my mother's womb, you have chosen me,"[2] I prayed and worshiped the Lord, rejoicing that we were expecting and that our baby was in my womb. By Sunday, we'd found out that our baby's heart had stopped beating. I struggled through these words but worshiped God that day too, praying through the tears, declaring that God is bigger than our present suffering. Although I could've found someone else to sing in my place, I don't regret worshiping through my suffering.

We're not insisting that you should push through every time the activity is ministry related. We simply want you to see that we have many opportunities to withdraw. Our hope is that you'll become aware of the emotions you're experiencing, reframe your thoughts, and take care of yourself. Sometimes that will mean saying no to things. Sometimes that will mean saying yes. The key is to understand your unmet needs and work to meet them one by one—whether at work or in a volunteer role.

God,

Grief is hard. Work is hard. I need You in the middle of it all. Go before me. Go behind me. Work through me.

Amen.

13 spiritual matters

GRIEF IMPACTS the way we view the world. It can especially alter how we look at spiritual matters, shifting our beliefs. When facing a loss, some people turn to God and find themselves more connected to Him than ever. And yet others feel distant from Him. And the same people may feel different during subsequent losses.

With the various losses we've faced, we've experienced God differently. I can vividly remember the day I found inappropriate images on Chuck's computer; I felt God's closeness in a way I never had before. I, Chuck, felt completely unworthy of God's love, but He felt close. I was also aware of my need to worship. During our seasons of miscarriage, we faced times when we felt unseen by God. We longed for Him to intervene, making us aware of His presence. When we lost babies, we sometimes felt like God wanted something from us that we couldn't provide. We knew God wanted us to draw close and be open to His voice. But we felt resistant, angry. We prayed fervently, yet we didn't get what we requested. In the first example we shared, there was sin in the camp, yet God felt nearby. In the second situation, we were trying to walk out Scripture and build God's kingdom during our loss, and God felt distant. This didn't make sense to us.

When reality is different from our idealistic expectations, we may experience dissonant thoughts. We face dissonance in many situations, but when our beliefs about God are challenged by a painful reality, we call it spiritual dissonance.[1] For example, you may have spent a lifetime believing God answers prayers, and most of the time, He has answered. But spiritual dissonance may occur when a prayer or several prayers seem to go unanswered or are answered differently than you wish.

We experienced spiritual dissonance. We spent years studying God's Word and preparing for battle. And then when we faced loss, grief, and transitions, there were times we expected God to feel near. But He didn't. We believe this experience of spiritual dissonance may cause many to turn away from God, but we hope you see that this experience happens to many people who follow Him. And we don't have to turn away. If we keep leaning in, pursuing Him, and connecting with others who love God, we can get to the other side with our spiritual views intact. But our beliefs are shaped by our thoughts, feelings, and emotions regarding our experiences. Sometimes it feels easier to change our beliefs about God rather than do the emotional, spiritual, and physical work necessary to explore the dissonance. Though this is tough work, it's not impossible.

As we analyzed our situation, we remembered that God's ways are higher than ours (Isa. 55:8–9) and chose to accept that, perhaps, He was teaching us to rely on Him even when we didn't feel His presence. He has given us His Word, and we can hold on to what it says, even when our emotions or our

> Spiritual dissonance: having two or more conflicting thoughts, feelings, or ideas about God.

reality scream that God is absent. As we look back on that time, we believe He was present. We choose to remember that we don't deserve God's presence, and He's worthy of our service even if we never see, feel, or hear from Him.

Sometimes it feels easier to change our beliefs about God rather than do the emotional, spiritual, and physical work necessary to explore the dissonance.

Have your views about God or spiritual matters changed since you faced loss? If you moved from being faith-filled to filled with anger or apathy, you're not alone. We felt that during our loss. God appeared cold, distant. If God were to have said something to us, we imagined He might have said, "Yep, these things happen. It's a fallen world." We often felt disappointed, like God cared less about us than we had previously believed. We prayed faith-filled prayers and even tried to have a *God-honoring* response to loss. We didn't ask God, "Why us?" We didn't believe God wanted our baby to die (some people may say to others that God *needed* an angel up in heaven). And neither of us turned to alcohol or other unhealthy behaviors; we ran to God. When we were sad, when we behaved negatively by being rude to people, we sought God's help. We apologized to others. But we were disappointed that we felt unable to feel close to Him at times. We really needed a hug.

We just wanted God to hold us, to be close and tell us we were going to be okay. But we didn't get that, at least not directly. We had some moments when we really struggled with it and became frustrated with God. We felt angry. We weren't angry that our babies had died; we were *sad* that they had died. I, Ashley, was *angry* that I had been faithful to God through it all and He had refused to come near to me when I needed Him most. I couldn't figure out why He chose to be distant.

But we kept coming back to the fact that we knew this wasn't His original plan. He wanted to be with us, and it was sin that drove us apart. In the final pages of the Bible, God says He will come to dwell with us again (Rev. 21:3). The longing of our hearts has been to be close to God. We're pretty sure that's pleasing to Him. It's how He made us; we were designed to desire His presence. We can survive spiritual dissonance by stopping our negative thoughts, looking to God's Word, and remembering that faith in God will resolve much of our dissonance.

Relationship with Our Creator

Relationships really aren't stagnant; we're either moving closer to each other or growing more distant. Are you moving closer to God or farther from Him? Maybe you find yourself angry at God. As discussed earlier, anger can be an appropriate emotion to experience in relationships. If you never experience any strong emotions such as anger, it's likely that you are not being super vulnerable in the relationship or are avoiding deep connection. We're not suggesting you need to live a chaotic life filled with daily anger, fear, and strife. But if you find yourself angry at God, simply explore why. Are you experiencing something similar to what we did? Have you prayed God would intervene? As you explore why you feel angry at God, be honest with Him. God may not speak to you in an audible voice. He did not speak plainly with us regarding our hurt either. You may experience silence. Or the Holy Spirit may speak to your heart as you read the Bible, engage in relationships, or spend time in nature.

Let's explore how God speaks to us in His Word. We can look at individuals in the Bible who may have felt that God was distant or silent. God told Abram, later known as Abraham, that he would have so many descendants they would be as numerous as the stars (Gen. 15:5), and then . . . crickets. It seemed God was much more silent than Abram wanted. If God had spoken more directly or more frequently, perhaps Sarai wouldn't have suggested that Abram sleep with her maidservant to produce children (Gen. 16:2–4). But He didn't. Why? We don't know for certain, but throughout Scripture, we see that God values faith. When Abram believed God would do what He had said, God credited Abram with righteousness (Gen. 15:6). God wants us to trust Him. During the daytime, when we can clearly see the sun, we don't have faith that the sun is shining. During the night, we have faith that the sun will shine again tomorrow.

Faith is not easy. "Faith is confidence in what we hope for and assurance about what we do not see" (Heb. 11:1 NIV). Faith requires having hope and assurance when we do not see. Isn't that beautiful? When we suffer—losing our babies, our jobs, our financial security, or our closest loved ones—and still trust our Creator, we are living by faith. And it's beautiful.

In Scripture, people are in awe of Job, not his wife. She asks why he doesn't just curse God and die (Job 2:9). He stays faithful to the end. We are drawn to heroes, to people who keep believing during tough times. This, too, is what our Creator does. Look at the Israelites. Or consider the book of Hosea. God continues to pursue people who have been unfaithful to Him. "If we are faithless, he remains faithful, for he cannot disown himself" (2 Tim. 2:13 NIV).

Faithless. Surely that doesn't describe us, does it? Hmm. Quietly, maybe even subconsciously, we blame God for our hurt. Knowing He has the power to stop suffering reveals that He chose not to, right? Perhaps. But it doesn't necessarily mean God desired the negative events to occur. Remember Job? The enemy approached God with a plan for suffering; God allowed it to bring glory to His name.

Sometimes comments offered by well-meaning Christians cause us to feel like God may want our suffering. When people say, "God has a bigger plan," it may feel hurtful. Of course He does, but the pain comes from feeling like the speaker is saying we should stop being selfish. That response may help the person feel spiritual, but it doesn't speak to the individual's pain.

Let's look at how these types of statements provoke spiritual dissonance. First, we agree; God has a bigger plan than just us. Second, when someone tells us this, it might invoke shame, causing us to note that the world is bigger than our feelings and experiences, and therefore, we should "suck it up." It can make us feel like God doesn't really care about our thoughts, feelings, or emotions, and He's concerned only with His plan. But this should feel conflicting, or dissonant, because God does care. He cares so much that He sent His son for us. So let's review this again.

God is faithful to His Word. In the beginning, He created the world. He chose to put a tree in the garden, giving Adam and Eve the privilege of being obedient or disobedient. Out of their disobedience, suffering was born. Daily, billions of people continue to follow Adam and Eve's example, disobeying God's instruction rather than following His plan. And the result of their free will is suffering in the form of divorce, job loss, distant relationships, communication problems, and more. God sent Jesus to rectify the situation and says He will dwell with us again someday (Rev. 21:3). He, too, wants something different. He wants union with us, connection to us, and for us to experience freedom from the bondage of sin.

When you feel strong emotions about your relationship with God, remind yourself that you're not alone. Take time to explore your thoughts, feelings, and emotions, praying God will help you resolve the dissonance.

Unanswered Prayers

What creates spiritual dissonance more than unanswered prayers? Perhaps stepping foot into church creates dissonance for you. It may trigger strong emotions, reminding us that God didn't answer our prayers. How might we feel when He doesn't answer as we wish? Perhaps we think the following:

1. My prayers are weak and therefore pointless.
2. God doesn't care about my needs.
3. God's not there.

Let's look at these feelings and consider how Scripture can help. When we feel our prayers are weak, we can acknowledge that our weakness is a small portion of the equation. God is powerful enough to do the healing work (Ps. 147:3) if we pray. James 5:16 tells us that the prayers of a righteous person are effective. When we feel that God doesn't care about our needs, we can read Psalms 13, 22, and 42 to hear how others felt alone but continued to worship God despite their hurt. And in Habakkuk 3:17–19, we see that some rejoiced in the Lord when they saw no food growing on their plants and no animals in their barns. God was with others even when they felt alone, and He showed up in the end. He is here for us as well. When we feel like God's not there, we can take comfort from Revelation 21:4, which states that when God returns, He will wipe away *every* tear. This shows that He sees us and He touches each tear, so He's in the moment even when we don't feel His presence. Ultimately, it's important to acknowledge our emotions so we can understand our unmet needs, pray, and find Scripture passages that reassure our faith in God.

Do you believe the Bible is true? Was God worthy of praise before the first sin? Yes, and He was worthy afterward as well.

He was worthy of praise while Jesus was being crucified, while Mary was crying, and while the disciples were hiding. He was worthy of praise before your suffering and in the middle of your sorrow. And after the dust has settled, He'll still be worthy. It doesn't mean it will always be easy, but we are not alone. Others have felt how we feel. Some have chosen to turn away, while others have dug deeper roots. Choose to dig deep roots.

If you need some support throughout this process, go to church, talk to a pastor, or call someone you look up to. Reach out to someone who will encourage you as you process spiritual matters. Keep in mind that even pastors and "spiritual" people are human, so they may not say all the right words. If they fail you, please remember that they also need a Savior; it does not mean God has failed you. We pray God will empower whoever you reach out to, using them to help you draw closer to God.

God,

Make me aware of ways my spiritual views have shifted. Put someone in my life to help me sort out my questions. Give me courage to take the steps You lay on my heart. You were worthy before I grieved. You are worthy amid my suffering. You will forever be worthy.

Amen.

PART 3

seeing my loved ones

Consider the ways your support system has shifted. As a result of your loss, you may look at your loved ones differently. Sometimes members of our support system step up and we feel more connected to our loved ones than ever. Other times we experience distance or poor support from those we wish would help us bandage our broken heart. We want to be seen, but it may feel uncomfortable to have people see us in our current state. First, we will learn how grief has impacted our relationships, and later, we will build skills that help us ask for what we need.

14 how grief impacts my intimate relationships

WHEN WE REFER to "intimate" relationships, we are speaking about relationships in which we are more *seen* than in our average relationships; for example, one's immediate family, spouse, and children are frequently quite intimate relationships. These individuals see us when we haven't brushed our teeth, and they often know us better than anyone else. So how does grief impact these relationships?

Since grief can trigger strong emotions, many of these may be stifled in everyday life, which can create a buildup aching to be expressed. This often results in displacement of emotion toward those with whom we share our most intimate relationships. Since we need the people closest to us during this season (and they continue needing us as well), it's important that we take care of ourselves so we can sustain these relationships. Grief can reduce our sense of mental stability; when we feel less stable, all our relationships can feel unsteady.

When this happens, we may withdraw. We may do this openly or subconsciously. When we feel less stable, we may recognize that we are ruining our relationships and decide to pull back, choosing to shut our loved ones out of our lives. This is a protective mechanism used to keep ourselves from suffering more pain. But when we engage in this behavior, the pain we attempt to protect ourselves from may become the source of new pain, loneliness, and depression. Instead, we must recognize that we are part of the solution. We can increase our mental stability by seeking professional help, talking with our closest friends and family, and pursuing God.

How Do I See My Loved Ones?

Often grief sends us into a negative space, impacting the way we see our loved ones. Our thoughts may shift from feeling loved and cared for by a significant other or child to feeling especially negative. Perhaps we even assume the person doesn't really care or would be better off without us. Our mental stability may shift because of triggers we have not processed. Do you know what actions by your significant other or children trigger you into a negative space? Process how you respond when this happens.

We remember feeling especially unstable about two to three days after we lost our babies. For the first day or so, we skipped some of our usual responsibilities like cooking and cleaning, which enabled us to snuggle, cry, or play. But once the regular responsibilities piled up and our kids began to fight, awful thoughts entered our minds: *We shouldn't be sad that we lost the baby. We cannot even keep two kids from fighting.* And then, tears. *We're failures and cannot control our kids. We cannot keep up with the laundry, our jobs, and all these emotions.* What do you think happened next? The desire to withdraw intensified.

How has grief impacted the way you see your most intimate relationships? If a statement, section, or chapter of this book has been especially insightful or even perplexing, give yourself permission to sit with the idea for a while. Pray. Invite God to reveal information about yourself to you. He knows you and your family better than you do and can help you navigate this season.

What If I Don't Want to Try?

Though our emotions may tell us we should give up, we don't have to obey them. We can listen to what needs they reveal should be met, but we don't have to let them rule our lives. Before we perform any action, we will experience emotions and thoughts. These are part of the alert system God created to help us engage in self-regulation. Take time to *see* yourself. Reflect on how you behave when you're the most mentally stable compared to when you're the least mentally stable. Complete the mental stability exercise on the next page to increase self-awareness so you can strengthen your relationships. Break down your daily behavior when you're at your best compared to when you're at your worst. Consider your daily hygiene habits, food intake, exercise, sleep practices, spiritual activities, work tendencies, friendship habits, etc.

> Though our emotions may tell us we should give up, we don't have to obey them.

For us, when we're the most mentally stable, we eat and sleep well, engage with God's Word, and invest in godly relationships, and we work hard both physically and mentally. When we feel less mentally stable, we're more likely to eat out rather than take time to plan and cook, we may stay awake too late, or we avoid building connections with our loved ones. When you become less mentally stable, what's the first thing to go? Exercise, time with God, healthy sleep practices? As you increase awareness about your own mental instability, you gain insight into how to build mental stability through your behavior, even

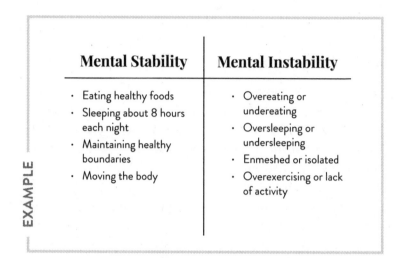

EXAMPLE

Mental Stability	Mental Instability
· Eating healthy foods · Sleeping about 8 hours each night · Maintaining healthy boundaries · Moving the body	· Overeating or undereating · Oversleeping or undersleeping · Enmeshed or isolated · Overexercising or lack of activity

Mental Stability	Mental Instability

when you don't feel like it. This greatly impacts your most intimate relationships.

What Happens If I Don't Try?

A beautiful thing about life is that we've been given free will. Therefore it's your choice to process your grief and the impact it has on your relationships. Of course, we hope to entice you to keep going. But you *are* going. You are still reading. You've made it this far, and you're here. Give yourself a little pat on the back. We just did. Really, we just gave ourselves some physical assurance. Join us!

Process what happens if you don't try, if you stop altogether and simply give up. Well, you'll grow apart from your loved ones. Since there are no stagnant relationships, you are getting either closer together or farther apart in all your relationships. Some studies have shown that when individuals face significant losses, it can take a toll on their marriage. A Harvard study revealed that when a man loses a job, he's at a 32 percent higher risk for divorce than someone who maintained full-time work.[1] And Dr. Katherine Gold reported that couples who faced miscarriage or stillbirth experience a significantly increased chance of divorce compared to couples who don't lose a child.[2] Do these studies imply doom? No way. Do they reveal that losses can greatly impact our closest relationships? Yes, certainly.

What Do I Hold On To?

As you explore how this loss has impacted your intimate relationships, we hope you hold on to the following ideas regarding your behavior:

- *It's normal to feel the need to stifle emotions or put on a strong face to barrel through a situation.* But doing so for too long will likely result in displaced emotions that tear apart the very relationships that give you hope to keep going in this tough season. Consider finding some ways to be honest about your struggles with someone at work, the gym, or wherever you feel the most pressure to "put on a strong face." Who's putting this pressure on you? Is it possible that it's you? And when you weigh the cost, is it worth hurting your marriage to keep your boss from knowing you feel a little more overwhelmed than normal? If people continue telling you how strong you are and your internal dialogue is shouting, "I'm lying," consider telling the person, "I don't feel strong. Actually, yesterday, I almost left a meeting because I was having a tough time. Thanks for seeing me." It may help your work relationship, but it will also free you up to feel mentally strong at home.

- *You have the power.* You can make the choice to invest in your mental stability and in your relationships. If you feel that you're lacking strength, lean into God's strength. "The Lord will fight for you; you need only to be still" (Exod. 14:14 NIV).

- *If you're in a negative space, you can make a manual reset, moving back toward a positive space.* It takes time, but you can do it.

- *There is a cost to allowing yourself to operate in shut-down mode for too long.* And one of the places that gets hit the hardest is your closest relationships. If you're aware that you're operating in "shut-down mode," create a deadline for yourself. For example, you could write in your calendar, "Shut-down mode ends today." This will remind you that you are working to heal. Remember, it's also okay to give yourself permission to readjust the deadline down the road; the goal is to keep moving.

As you explore your intimate relationships, take courage. You're doing hard work that will help you leave a legacy. Change will cost you something. As you invite God into your healing journey, prepare for the Holy Spirit to nudge you to love, forgive, and lean into your loved ones when your human tendency may be to lean out.

God,

I don't want to remain shut down to You or my loved ones. Help me lean into You so that my relationships will honor You.

Amen.

15 | how others respond to my loss

HOW HAVE YOUR LOVED ONES responded to your loss? Consider the ways others have finished the sentence "My loved ones _____."

My loved ones <u>have no idea I'm hurting</u>.

My loved ones <u>are very supportive</u>.

My loved ones <u>don't know what to say</u>.

My loved ones <u>think I should stop complaining, suck it up, and get back to normal</u>.

Contemplate how you would finish the sentence "My loved ones _____." Can you recognize which of the statements above are from individuals in a positive space versus a negative space? It's possible that the same person, while in a positive space, could say that their family is supportive, but on a tough day, while in a negative space, would think that their loved ones care very little. Therefore, although our support system may be lacking at times, it's important to acknowledge that there may be other times when we are simply in a negative space and not allowing our loved ones to help us.

Of course, all of us would like to feel that our loved ones are supportive. Take a moment to ponder this question: "Have I asked my loved ones for what I need? Can *I* even identify what I need?" Ehh. Tough, right? If we're unable to express what we need, it's difficult to expect others to meet our needs.

Whether our loved ones offer exactly what we need or fail to help in any way, we can still get our needs met. Thankfully, if we don't feel that we have supportive loved ones, we can build relationships with others who will help us. We can also repair some relationships that may need mending. The first step is to explore the support system we have already built.

My Loved Ones Are with Me

Make a list of the people who are in your corner. Feel free to use the margins to jot down names of people in your support system. If you need help with this, pick up your phone and look at the number of people with whom you have communicated via text, email, and/or social media within the past few days. Then choose a few relationships to explore and identify who initiated the conversation. As you work to increase your support system, choose to pursue a conversation with someone you want to be closer to, perhaps someone who has already invested in you in the past. It takes two people to keep a relationship strong. In her book *Find Your People*, Jennie Allen encourages us to go first.[1] Don't wait for someone else to take the first step. Initiate, even if no one else ever seems to.

As you think about who's on the journey with you, take a moment to be thankful. Grief tends to tell us that we are alone, that no one cares for us. Fight back. Remind yourself of the people who care for you. Has someone reached out to you? In our experiences, we tend to initiate much more than we receive invites or encouraging words. Though it can be easy to get into a negative space about it, we try to be thankful that we can invest in others. Today is a good day to connect with people you love. Don't wait until you "feel" like it.

If you perceive that you don't have people who love you, think about relationships that used to be strong. What happened? Perhaps you have some relationships that are not "current." Years ago, at a relationship training workshop, we heard this idea of being current. If we are current with our loved ones, we have worked to resolve all issues and are not holding cognitive weapons of destruction that serve as barriers to connection.

Early in our marriage, we found ourselves having many discussions about laundry. If I was unhappy about laundry, I'd feel more impatient when Chuck returned home a little later than expected. It's amazing how feelings of disrespect in one area can compound and build resentment in other areas as well. This is why it's important to communicate our needs. If we don't feel current in a relationship, it's our responsibility to communicate. It's possible that our loved ones don't know what we are upset about and need clear communication. And sometimes we need repeated communication.

My Loved One Is Also Grieving

Do you ever feel negative emotions about your negative emotions? For example, you may feel guilty for being sad because your loved one has also faced loss and you feel pressure to be strong for them. This can cause you to conceal your emotions, hoping that burying them will make them go away. But instead, burying your pain plants seeds of hurt that you don't want to grow into trees of devastation.

Consider two of the many ways you may respond if a loved one grieves differently than you. You may try to keep it together around them because they hog all the emotions for the whole family. Or maybe you're the one with all the feels. You look at your family, who seem so calm, and their serenity induces rage within you.

Have you ever taken time to ask yourself, "Why does it make me so mad that they respond differently from me?" Sometimes we have felt angry because others seem to find it easy to respond in ways that are unnatural to us. We've been upset that people were silent when we desperately needed them to ask us how we were. We felt this was the "elephant in the room" but later realized it might've been our elephant—and in fact, it was an invisible elephant we brought into the room and then expected our family to address. They didn't. They couldn't. They didn't see the elephant. And since we didn't tell them the elephant was there, they thought we were fine, handling life well. We felt alone. Everyone may have felt a little bit confused but shrugged it off. Without communication about our needs, we drift apart.

Anger

In the previous paragraph, we shared personal examples of feeling angry about our loved ones' behavior. When we get angry, sometimes we build walls that separate us from our loved ones. This protective wall is built of unstable bricks, where each brick represents hurt from a difficult situation. From the outside, people see anger. When we look deeper, we may find vulnerable feelings such as weakness, jealousy, sorrow, or inadequacy. Many emotions lie beneath our anger. What's behind yours?[2] Let's deconstruct the walls built to protect.

When we felt angry at people who responded differently from us, jealously was sometimes behind it. Partly, we wished we could be more like certain family members. But why would we experience anger if our true emotion was jealousy? Let's consider what jealousy evokes in us. Hmm. Are you squirming

Anger Wall

in your seat yet? Most of us don't like to be jealous. We don't want to be weak and desire to move away from this emotion. When we are angry, we feel justified, powerful, right. So jealousy reveals weakness, while anger brings a sense of power. Now it makes sense why people choose anger over jealousy.

We can take time to be honest about our emotions, asking, "What other emotions do I feel right now?" or "Is my anger covering another emotion?" Then we can directly address our unmet needs instead of tearing apart our most important relationships. Have we told you that *we* are still works in progress? Although we teach these concepts, we haven't completely mastered them. We still spiral downward and develop negative behavior. Yet when we practice healthy habits, we get better and can recognize our own negative patterns.

Behind our anger lay unmet needs. We really wanted to feel seen by our family. We're still sorting out exactly what we felt in different situations, but we believe our pride got in the way. What if I, Ashley, had fallen into a family member's arms and cried? Instead, I wanted someone else to be vulnerable, inviting me to be seen. But needs don't just go away because people don't meet them. We simply try to meet them in other ways. We adjust our beliefs, telling ourselves we will be fine. And sometimes we are. Until we aren't. If we're not all right, we can learn to become okay with letting go of our pride and telling our loved ones, "I'm hurting." And then maybe, just hug them.

> Needs don't just go away because people don't meet them.

You know another thing we've learned? In our family, we often want more than we get. We love each other very much, but each person has different needs, and we're frequently assessing whether we think others care about our needs. In the end, most of us would like to be closer.

Several years ago, my dad had surgery for prostate cancer. After the procedure, I remember standing in his small hospital room and feeling connected to him; he wanted to hold our hands. What was most memorable about that experience? Worry? No. Were we thankful for cancer? No. But years later, I'm glad my dad asked me to hold his hand. Maybe we've got it all wrong. Maybe our pride breeds depression and loneliness. And maybe our pride keeps others from feeling cherished and needed. Lord, help us! Why do we feel so compelled to hide our needs? Perhaps if we go ahead and ask for what we need, we will find ourselves in a positive space, able to complete the statement "My loved ones _____" with positive sentiments.

Now, many of these techniques we've shared are simple. But they can be tough to live out. We aren't perfect at living them out either. And we're aware that we will continue needing these tools to help us when we face future losses. So if you don't find this stuff comes easily for you, it's okay. Keep going. We've been amazed at how God has worked in us over the years, but we've also had plenty of moments when we sat in sorrow, thinking about how far we had to go. The key is to keep moving and continue running to God and your loved ones.

God Is a Loved One

When we asked you to fill in the blank regarding loved ones, it may not have crossed your mind to consider God as a loved one. But does He love you? Yes! And He can sustain you. So how do you fill in the blank regarding your Heavenly Father?

God loves me but doesn't feel close.

God doesn't care for me.

God holds me.

"God _____."

Is God there for you in the ways you need Him to be? Have you spoken with Him about your needs and wishes? Consider how the following verses sit with you:

> God's way is perfect.
>> All the LORD's promises prove true.
>> He is a shield for all who look to Him for
>>> protection. (Ps. 18:30)

> God is our refuge and strength,
>> an ever-present help in trouble. (Ps. 46:1 NIV)

If you struggle with these verses, you may be in a negative space with God. Be honest with God about your unmet needs. Tell Him that it's hard for you to read the verses above because it feels like He's anything but present. If you need to, reread these verses or look up some others that have triggered hurt. Talk to God about it. Explore what unmet needs might be triggering strong emotions for you. After you've processed for a while, if you can, tell God that you commit to Him—even in His silence. Remind yourself that God is worthy of your praise, even when life is difficult. Talk to God honestly, then listen for His guidance. He's eager to help you.

God,
 I want to be strong. Help me become like Job, who served You even when he lost everything [Job 13:15]. Help me submit my unbelief to You, knowing that You see my heart [Mark 9:24].
 Amen.

16 my altered support system

WHEN WE EXPERIENCE LOSS, we often lose members of our support system. If we quit or lose a job or if a close coworker gets promoted, our work support system may be altered. This also happens if we move across the country for a loved one to pursue their career goals. Though we may be able to stay connected to individuals through technology, it's important to acknowledge that our support system has been altered.

Have you recently lost members of your social, work, or family support system? Take a few minutes and reflect on the list you began in the last chapter. If you find yourself thinking, *I've got no friends*, two things are possible: 1) you might be in a negative space, or 2) you have not spent time building relational wealth.[1] Either way, there is hope. If you're in a negative space, ask yourself one of these questions: "On a happy day, who would I like to spend time with?" or "If I were in a positive space, who would I say was in my support system?" You can also make a note to come back to this activity on another day.

If you haven't spent time building relational wealth, take a closer look at how you can develop your support system.

Simply put, relational wealth means you're wealthy with friendships, having many people you could call on in a difficult season. If your support system has been altered and you're doing okay, chances are you're relationally wealthy.

How Loss Can Lead To Relational Distance

Sometimes when we face loss, we may experience grief because we feel distant from the members of our support system. What could be happening here? Remember that relationships are not stagnant; we're moving either closer together or farther apart. If you feel *distant* from your support system, this is likely due to one of three main possibilities: 1) the other person could be withdrawing consciously or unconsciously, 2) you could be withdrawing consciously or unconsciously, or 3) neither of you are doing enough to sustain the relationship, so the space between you is growing wider. If either or both of you are living in protective mode, trying to survive rather than investing in relationships, you may not mean to withdraw, but that's the result.

> Remember that relationships are not stagnant; we're moving either closer together or farther apart.

Let's walk through some examples. With the pandemic came fear. From sickness to judgment, punishment to rejection, people moved from fear to fear. Since people like to avoid fear, many entered survival mode for a while, connecting with their support system using only technology. But for most, this was not enough. Face-to-face human interaction was needed. If there were members of our support system who were unable or unwilling to connect, our support system was altered. When kids were not able to go to school, their support systems were altered. When parents had to become teachers and continue working, their support systems were altered. When adult children couldn't go to the nursing home to see their parents, support systems were altered.

Altered support systems aren't new. People *are* resilient, and they march on. But it's okay to acknowledge that there have been many changes, and those changes might elicit strong emotions. Can you accept yourself, knowing that your feelings are to be expected, given the circumstances?

Miscarriage and Our Support System

When we faced miscarriage, our baby had not yet become part of our support system. Yet we experienced shifts in our relationships. We felt that there were some people we could talk to while there were others who didn't seem to understand. One of our friends was so thoughtful; she purchased a gift box from Hope Mommies,[2] an organization developed to support people facing the loss of their babies.

To help us process, we sought out others who had walked our path. We inquired about their losses. We shared our hurts. I, Chuck, recall one of the first times I shared with a mentor and friend about losing our baby. The two of us were golfing, and I knew he and his wife had struggled in a similar way. As he began to share, it hit me like a ton of bricks. I realized I was not alone, and it was not only okay but also right for men to feel the pain of losing a child before they are born. My friend shared details regarding the hospital visit where he held his son for the first and last time. He cried. I teared up as well. This was a turning point for me in understanding grief, and grief as a man. We were not created to struggle alone.

Walking with others is crucial. In addition to people, there are great resources available that can provide support.

Resources Can Be Part of Our Support System

We've used several resources to strengthen our faith over the years. The YouVersion Bible App has been one of the most influential tools we've found. When we lost babies, we completed reading plans on the topic. I, Ashley, read a plan called "Finding God in Your Miscarriage" by Brittany Rust that was especially encouraging to me because Brittany was incredibly vulnerable regarding her suffering.[3] We also love RightNow Media and watched a video series on miscarriage that provided emotional support. Consider the ways you consume content. Where do you seek entertainment? There are podcasts, social media groups, and local meetings for so many types of loss. If you're in need of support, there are ways to begin building connection today.

Reflect on the ways your support system has been altered. How can you continue to develop relational wealth? Consider which resources can help build your relational and mental stability so you can also support those you love when they face difficulties. Remember that Jesus has overcome the world (John 16:33), so He can help secure your world, including your support system, even when it's shifted a bit.

> God,
>
> Help me see those who are for me. Sometimes I feel alone, but I acknowledge that my negative space assumptions can be wrong. Help me build relational and mental stability.
>
> Amen.

17 when my support system doesn't meet my needs

BEFORE WE CAN THINK DEEPLY about whether our support system meets our needs, it is helpful to be aware of our needs. Have you taken time to use the Three A's to Change? First, become *aware* of your needs. Second, *assess* what has and has not helped you meet those needs. And third, *act*. When your support system doesn't meet your needs, consider ways you can take action to meet your needs in a different way.

As we walk through some practical steps for how to get our needs met, we want to share a story about how our support system didn't meet our needs and how I, Ashley, reacted very poorly, creating deeper wounds when I really needed healing.

Just a few days after we found out one of our babies' hearts had stopped beating, we were scheduled to go camping with our family. We didn't seriously consider staying home because we believed community would help us, and we had two young boys who loved to play. We didn't want them to miss out on time with their cousins when they had just lost the hope of a future younger sibling. So we went. Time crawled as kids rode bikes and played with sticks. As we sat in lawn chairs around a fire, one by one, more family members arrived. Most of them said nothing about our loss. While on a walk, one asked us how we were. We felt seen. But as the hours ticked on, we felt more and more alone. We wondered, *Why didn't our family acknowledge our loss?* Typically, one of the things we love about camping is the fact that time seems to slow down, but in our loss, we had coped by keeping busy. We wanted to slow down and share how we felt, but we didn't initiate the conversation. When others avoided the topic, we assumed they just wanted to have fun and not invest in us.

We were a little quieter than usual. The next day, we went boating. When everyone boarded the boats, there were not enough life jackets for all the kids. As a mom, I was worried. Everyone else seemed to see minimal risk, but I saw death. I had just lost a child, and I didn't want to lose another one. But I also couldn't handle the thought of one of the kids being without a life jacket either. I admit I probably made it a bigger deal than it needed to be, but again, in my heart, I felt unseen. It didn't seem like they took our loss seriously, or they wouldn't have been asking us to risk our children's lives by boarding a boat without a life jacket. In time, I settled down and tried to relax and have fun.

With about twenty people in two boats, the experience was a bit overwhelming. People had different needs and wishes. We were supposed to pick up a Jet Ski and some more life jackets, but there was very little communication about how and when these things would happen. This left us feeling less in control than we wished to feel.

Eventually we ended up at a place where people could cliff dive. My memory is a bit foggy about what exactly happened to trigger an explosion, but when someone was dismissive about getting life jackets, I lost it. I yelled about how the family had not communicated the entire trip and dropped the f-bomb in front of the kiddos and family. (For the record, we don't swear in our home, so this was quite out of character.) I cried out that our baby had died and began punching a chair. Then, feeling embarrassed and trapped, thoughts raced through my mind about how to escape. I considered jumping out of the boat, but when I realized it would likely result in having to get picked up by the family, the option felt less desirable.

I cried harder than Chuck remembers seeing me cry during any other time. He felt helpless, unsure how to support me. The boat remained quiet until we came to shore, where we exited for lunch. I apologized to the family, and someone told me they felt like they had acknowledged our pain when they hugged us, citing they didn't want to ask about our loss, fearing it could make things worse.

All right, you can see how our support system didn't meet our needs, but we were still responsible for our own behavior. What could we have done to help us recognize that we had unmet needs? Let's use the three A's. First, were we *aware* of whether we had any signals telling us we were not okay? The day before, we were having a tough time. We knew we didn't feel supported. The lack of life jackets was another trigger.

Now, let's *assess* what we did and what we could have done. 1) We could have gotten off the boat when there were not enough life jackets for everyone. 2) We could have given ourselves permission to open up and ask for someone to listen. We believed people didn't care or they would have asked. This simply isn't always true. We've met very few people who feel comfortable asking others about their loss; most people report feeling uncertain about what to say or ask in response to grief.

The final A is to *act*. How do we act differently because of what we have learned? We try to listen to our bodies, understanding that we always receive some alerts that we are not okay before we behave in a negative manner. Now we give ourselves permission to exit the situation to avoid acting this way.

Ideally, each of us would live with amazing, supportive people who anticipate our needs and help us through difficult times without needing to be asked for anything. But that is an ideal, not a realistic expectation. As we have developed and processed Switch Theory, we've reflected on past events to better understand our behavior. When we lost our baby right before that camping trip, we experienced an automatic switch to a negative space. Although we fought to reside in a positive space, we kept feeling catapulted to a negative space. We had wrongly thought that time with our family would help us move back to a positive space. But we attended the camping trip with unmet needs. It was unrealistic to think that anything other than addressing our unmet needs would wholly make us feel better.

Have you felt unseen, wishing people would do something to meet your needs? Back in chapter 11, we discussed how confusing it can be when we don't accurately communicate our feelings. When we are in a positive space, we don't always notice that someone else is in a negative one. Or we may recognize that they're in a negative space and not know how to make it better, so we remain quiet. Consider committing to communicating your needs with someone in your support system so they don't have to guess how to help you.

> It was unrealistic to think that anything other than addressing our unmet needs would wholly make us feel better.

As we reflect on why we didn't ask for something from our family, we don't have a clear answer. But partly, I reacted poorly because I felt they didn't care (which identifies that I was in a negative space because I know my family cares deeply for me). Do you want to know another part of the equation that's harder for me to admit? Pride. I didn't want to ask for what I needed. That felt weak or as if I was trying to take the spotlight or get attention. I didn't want either of those; I just wanted to feel better. What if I had just whispered to someone that I was having a hard time and asked if they would pray for me? Whew. Wouldn't that have been such a better place to cry rather than on the boat? But I didn't do that. Why? It didn't come to mind. My guess is that my pride kept it from coming. Lord, help me be better. Help me run to You. I pray that over you as well. May God help you recognize your needs and give you the courage to reach out to someone who cares for you.

Your Support System May Be Doing Their Best

It's also beneficial to recognize that members of your support system may be doing the best they can. And sometimes, that's still not enough. We can feel tempted to have a pity party, but we want to challenge you to resist doing this for too long. It's okay to grieve that our support system may not be there for us in the ways we wish they would be, but let's get to working. After we evaluate whether we have one or two people we could speak with, let's ask for what we need. We're going to dive into this in the next chapter.

God Is Part of Your Support System

Do you recognize God as part of your support system? When people say the wrong things, do you turn to God's Word for support? He speaks to us through the Bible, providing hope. The Holy Spirit produces love when we have brokenness, joy when we have emptiness, peace when we feel unsure, patience when we would rather have immediate answers, kindness when we feel like exploding on people who fail to meet our needs, goodness even in adversity, faithfulness when we feel like giving up, gentleness rather than anger, and self-control so that we do not act on every thought that enters our minds (Gal. 5:22–23). After all, do we consider people faithful when they've only experienced blessing? No, we see people who endure as faithful.

Oh, how we need God's Spirit to fill us each day. On our best days, we still fall short. We should bear more fruit. Yet we lean into grace. God's grace is sufficient for us. We can continue to lean into His power. For His power is made perfect in our weakness (2 Cor. 12:9).

Use the Three A's to Change to understand your needs (be *aware* of your met and unmet needs, *assess* healthy ways you could meet these needs, and *act*). Then consider whether your support system can assist you as you work to meet your needs. Bring God into this process, trusting Him as the Healer, the One who can meet your needs better than any human.

God,

   I'm sorry for thinking that anything other than You can fulfill me. Give me patience with my friends and family, as all of us are broken and in need of a Savior. Forgive me for expecting my friends and family to provide what only You can offer.

                       Amen.

18 | asking for what I need

DO YOU EVER HAVE a tough time asking for what you need? Or maybe it's just us. If you truly don't have a difficult time asking for what you need, you may not need this chapter for yourself personally. But we hope you'll keep reading, because many of your coworkers, loved ones, and neighbors may not find it easy to ask for what they need. After reading this, you'll be able to better empathize with them.

In chapter 17, we shared one reason I, Ashley, found it difficult to ask for what I needed. Do you remember my struggle? *Pride.* Eek. It's not fun to admit, especially considering that overall, neither of us considers ourselves prideful. But isn't that the human condition? If you struggle with pride and find it difficult to share, vulnerability is the antidote. When we are vulnerable, we allow people to see past our outer facade. When we choose to be vulnerable and ask for what we want, we tend to feel seen.

The Ask

By our third loss, we had learned that some of the ways we coped with previous losses had left us feeling lonely. We asked someone close to us if they would come to our home and listen. They did. We found that this encounter not only brought stability to that relationship, but it also helped us feel more mentally stable in other relationships as well. It's interesting how empowering it can be to take our unmet needs to the Lord, asking Him to help us. And sometimes He may show us who to invite into our loss. You know? Maybe this was one of the ways God was close to us, working in our grief. Though we didn't feel Him every day in the same ways we were used to, as we reflect on our loss, we can see more ways He was working, nonetheless.

But What If It Turns Out Poorly?

When a few of our friends or family responded to our losses by saying things like "God's got a plan," we heard, "God planned for our babies to die." Since this didn't sit well with our hearts, we began thinking, praying, and reading God's Word in search of answers. We believe God is sovereign and in control of the world, meaning He could control our thoughts and actions. But since we see that God implores people to change their ways and follow Him, we can safely assume that not every action that occurs in life makes God happy. So although people say, "God's got this" or "God's got a plan" and that may be true, it can be hurtful to someone grieving because they mistake the loss as divine punishment, teaching, or prescription from God. If reaching out brings more hurt or if someone offers you solace or spiritual advice that doesn't sit well with you, be curious about it. It may not be as spiritual or as helpful as they had hoped. And it may not mean you're unspiritual or lacking wisdom. Consider the story of Joseph and his brothers in the Bible. They hurt him, but Joseph replied, "You intended to harm me, but God intended it for good to accomplish what is now being done, the saving of many lives" (Gen. 50:20 NIV). If God can use what was intended to harm Joseph, God can use accidental insensitive comments to help us draw closer to God too.

> "You intended to harm me, but God intended it for good to accomplish what is now being done, the saving of many lives" (Gen. 50:20 NIV).

As you look at your losses, hold on to Romans 8:28, which says, "In all things God works for the good of those who love him, who have been called according to his purpose" (NIV). We want to look to God, but that doesn't prevent hurtful comments from deepening our wounds.

People ask many hurtful questions or make harmful comments to grieving individuals. Let's explore a few reasons why this happens. First, here are some common phrases people offer to comfort those who are grieving:

1. God must have needed an angel.
2. God won't allow you to go through more than you can handle.
3. Doesn't it make you grateful for the kids you have?
4. When God closes a door, He always opens a window.
5. There's something (or someone) better out there for you.
6. There's a reason for everything.
7. Time will heal.
8. I'm sorry (and then proceed to tell you about another loss they've experienced or heard about recently).
9. It's crazy how many people experience miscarriages. I never realized how common it is. (In the blank, insert other losses such as divorce, death, etc.)

10. How far along were you? Are you going to try again? Did he die suddenly? How old was she?
11. They are in a better place.

What's behind these questions and comments? Most people mean well. They're not vindictive or evil, hoping to hurt someone while they're low. Why do people continue asking crappy questions of those they love and want to help? Reread numbers 1–7 above. Do you see a theme? With each of these questions or comments, the speaker feels they are providing an answer of sorts. Numbers 1, 2, and 4 are spiritual answers, so it's possible the person feels a need to be spiritual or to help you be spiritual. Unintentionally, though, it can inflict pain on you and encourage questioning in a season when godly comfort is more valuable. Numbers 3, 5–7, and 11 are hopeful comments that try to direct the grieving person to something good. These comments can cause the grieving individual to feel as if hurting is unacceptable and needs to be hidden or quickly and quietly recovered from.

In the past decade, we've noticed that many people respond to comments about loss with other comments about loss (number 8). We especially see this happen at funerals (discussed in chapter 10) when people experience grief triggers. So if someone responds to your expression of grief by sharing about their own loss, it's possible that your loss triggered something in them. If they fail to support you in that moment, they may have their own grief work that needs to be done.

When people make comments about how much grief or loss they see around them, it seems to trivialize our loss (number 9). The person's goal may be to help us feel seen, but often negative feelings flood us as we feel that our hurt is drowned out by hurt around us. We may also feel guilty for struggling, given that so many others have it worse than us.

Lastly, why do people insist on asking questions such as "How old was he?" or "Did you have any idea they were having an affair?" These types of questions appear self-seeking. The inquirer may be looking for information to know how much empathy to provide. Seemingly, if the person was elderly, less empathy is needed. If the gender of the baby was known, more empathy is given. When we are asked these types of questions, it can make us feel like the person is comparing losses rather than providing care.

Regardless, we don't think any of these responses are meant to inflict wounds. But it's appropriate to recognize and share that they are more hurtful than helpful. Why, though, do we often keep these thoughts to ourselves? In the moment, we may feel unspiritual, guilty, or too emotionally exhausted to recognize or name what is going on. But now that you're away from the immediate situation, take time to reflect on comments that keep looping through your mind. It's likely they're on replay because your mind is trying to reconcile dissonance. Write down the statements. Take them to God. Search Scripture for answers. Talk to other godly people. Ask yourself, "Was it personal? Did the person mean to hurt me, or am I easily triggered because of unmet needs?"

> "Was it personal? Did the person mean to hurt me, or am I easily triggered because of unmet needs?"

Different Strokes for Different Folks

We are individuals with different needs. Some of us are great listeners, some overshare, and others may cringe at either of those options. But all of us need to feel loved and accepted. When we face loss, we may experience a heightened sense of awareness regarding our relational needs. Take time to know yourself so you will be aware of your needs.

We all need relationships. None of us is exempt. God made us to need one another (1 Cor. 12:12–27). Though it may be difficult to acknowledge at times, it's probably best if we go ahead and admit our dependence on God and others. We know, that whole pride thing can get in the way of this! But the reward is great: deep, meaningful relationships.

How do we develop close relationships? Some would suggest getting a mentor. Perhaps you were like me, Chuck, and grew up with multiple mentor figures in your life, or maybe you relate more to me, Ashley, who never had a specific person I considered a mentor. Either way, most people find it a bit awkward to ask someone, "Will you be my mentor?" Take solace that we won't prescribe that here. Instead, reflect on some of the people you've encountered in the past six months. If you've thought, *I'd love to spend more time with this person!* then invite them to take a walk, play racquetball, or go out for coffee. If you're looking to grow in a specific area of your life, consider building a relationship with someone a little farther along in the process. If you lost a loved one to death or divorce, reach out to someone who has faced a similar loss and could listen. As you share, hopefully you'll feel seen in new ways and develop deeper relationships.

Building Strong Relationships Takes Time

If you feel that your support system is lacking, acknowledge this. It takes time to develop strong relationships. In fact, the best practice is to build meaningful relationships when you're healthy and feeling mentally stable. Then these relationships will be established when one of you faces adversity. If your support system is not super stable right now, consider ways you can invest in new relationships. In your time of loss, seek support from a pastor or counselor in addition to friends, colleagues, family, and neighbors.

Although people want to have strong relationships, very few report having meaningful conversations.[1] This doesn't have to be the case. If you're concerned about the words a person may say in response to your loss, consider asking them to just listen. Earlier we mentioned how we asked a talkative member of our support system to do this. Here's the formula we followed: We grieved. Someone wanted to help. We asked for what we needed. They did it. Although it's not a perfect formula, you might be surprised by what you get if you simply ask for what you need. Try it!

We are capable of so much more than we think. As you explore why you may forego meaningful conversations, we pray that you'll invite God to give you courage to ask deep questions about faith, grief, and love.

> God,
> You created me to be in relationship. Forgive me for expecting people to meet my needs without my communication. Grant me courage to ask for what I need.
> Amen.

19 | creating an exit strategy

WE'VE ALL BEEN THERE, wanting to escape, wishing words would stop flowing out of someone's mouth so we could make our exit. But we stay. We endure. And later, we regret it, wondering why we didn't take care of ourselves at the moment. If that hasn't happened to you, you may be the one making others wish they could escape! An exit strategy is a mental plan to take care of ourselves in social settings where we may experience unmet needs.

Think of some of your worst moments in life. If you had developed an exit strategy, it may have been possible for you to avoid either being hurt or hurting others. What will you do if you get to work, vacation, or church and realize you're not okay? Having an exit strategy is especially helpful when you first experience loss because a plan pushes you to think through your self-care needs. Additionally, anticipating your needs in advance may allow you to stay. Perhaps creating an exit strategy is more like creating a stay strategy.

If you plan to go anywhere difficult, think about it ahead of time and explore your fears. Consider the worst-possible outcome. It might sound a bit drab, but if you think about the worst scenario, you will be prepared. And how often have our *worst* fears actually happened? Be careful not to dramatize or dwell on the possibilities; use this as an exercise. For example, let's say you're considering going to a funeral, but you're afraid you will break down because your grief is still fresh and you haven't been to a funeral since your loss. Now that you're *aware* of what could happen in a worst-case scenario, you can develop an exit strategy.

> An exit strategy is a mental plan to take care of ourselves in social settings where we may experience unmet needs.

You can plan by *assessing* your needs using the following questions:

- How difficult do I anticipate it will be?
- What will trigger strong emotions (smells, memories, etc.)?
- Will loved ones go with me? Will I receive support?
- Can I ask for what I need before I go?
- How long do I think it would be good for me to be there?
- What can I do to help myself feel safe to exit, if needed?

Once you've thought through some of the answers to the above questions, you can move toward *action*. Yes, it will still be tough, but knowing the challenges you may face, preparing for them, and creating an exit strategy should help you feel a little bit more in control. Know that although you've planned, it's likely you'll still have unpredictable encounters. Be proud of yourself for doing hard things. You'll be stronger for it.

When Gathering Hurts

Have you heard enough of our failures through our losses? Okay. We will share another one. One Thanksgiving, we were gathered at a family member's home to share a meal together. Over thirty people were in the house, more than half of whom were boys under age thirteen, so you can imagine the noise. One of our family members shared about their divorce. A while later, our boys were roughhousing and one of our kids' glasses were broken. This was a trigger. We had corrected the boys multiple times, and this was the second time our son's glasses had been broken in a short period of time due to playing roughly. And I, Ashley, admittedly responded poorly. I embarrassed my child by announcing to everyone that he had been disobedient and broken his brother's glasses. This led to an argument with my mom, who wanted to assure me that it was not as big of a deal as I felt it was. We were both distressed about a divorce in the family, resulting in tension, misunderstanding, and hurtful words exchanged between us.

So why did all this occur? First, it's complicated, so we're not sure it's possible to understand completely, but we have spent a great amount of time evaluating the experience. We don't think either of us had an exit strategy planned. Do you remember HALT? Don't get too hungry, angry, lonely, or tired? Well, we added another *H*. Don't get too *hot*. In addition to being angry with our kids' misbehavior and our family's failed relationships, we felt quite hot. We didn't take care of our basic needs or listen to our emotional alert system. Had we known we were about to engage in regretful behavior, we would have stepped outside to cool off and create an exit strategy.

Since then, we have tried to prepare an exit strategy for when others are in control of the environment. We remind each other that we can leave at any point and try to think about our needs in advance. Sometimes we pack snacks to avoid feeling "hangry." We also prioritize getting rest, listening to our alert systems, and engaging in self-care so we will be emotionally strong in general but especially during times of tension.

Grief and the Family

Contemplate this saying: "We hurt the ones we love the most." People sometimes use this saying to excuse bad behavior, but there's some truth in this phrase. When we love deeply, we should feel safe and able to let our guard down. And when our guard is down, we speak a bit more freely. This is a good thing until we say something hurtful. Now, we grieve how we sometimes feel guarded around family. After a couple of negative experiences within a few years, we are motivated to work diligently to avoid these types of situations. We want to feel free to be ourselves, yet when we're hurting, we may react harshly. This causes tension. Have you ever acted similarly? Maybe you can't get close to people, and you're not sure why. Maybe you've built so many protective walls that you've blocked yourself off from others.

As you continue seeking the Lord regarding your needs, consider if you should create an exit strategy. What will your strategy look like? Perhaps you will make a mental note that if you get too hungry, angry, lonely, tired, or _____ (fill in the blank with anything that can set you off), you will exit the room to take a break. If you're able to use coping mechanisms to reset, then returning may be a great idea. If not, it may be time to leave the situation entirely, before you feel overwhelmed. Remember, you're in charge of you. You can create an exit strategy based on your unique needs and situations.

Consider a scenario where you're deciding if you should spend time with family or stay home. Picture yourself sitting alone while your family is gathered without you. How will you feel? Ask God for clarity as you process how to best meet your needs. On one extreme, withdrawing too much can breed depression, but it can also be harmful to go and then damage relationships. When we engage in self-care practices, we build mental stability that enables us to connect with others and also take care of ourselves.

When the two of us evaluate what happened in a couple of the worst experiences in our lives, they all involve family. Why? Because we are close with our family and spend more time being ourselves with them. They also see us more than others. And even among our families, we may feel unseen. We're sure they do too. But we want to see them. And we think your loved ones want to see you as well.

Thanks for listening to our struggles. We pray God uses our willingness to share our weaknesses. There is hope, even when we are broken. Invite God into the process, helping you understand how to create an exit strategy when needed.

God,

Help me stay when I need to stay. Help me take a break or leave when needed so I can realign my focus on You. Equip me to return after I've spent time with You so I can maintain community.

Amen.

reframing grief

seeing grief from a new perspective

In parts 1 to 3, you examined yourself closely, thinking about what you need and identifying who's in your corner. You began the process of reframing by building awareness. To move toward action as we reframe, we'll look for good in difficult situations. We'll work to shift our perspective and practice thought-stopping techniques, using God's Word to help us move toward a positive space. Ready?

20 recall the good

YOUR MIND MAY DRIFT toward recalling either the positive or negative activities from the day. It's possible that your mood impacts this tendency. We find that when we're in a negative space, we may also think negatively about work, family, faith, and other aspects of our lives. And when we're in a positive space, we're more optimistic about solving problems and at times even overlook negative encounters with little effort.

Sometimes we slowly move into a negative space, and other times, we experience an automatic switch, feeling catapulted into a negative space. This movement can result from a sudden loss or a series of unmet expectations in life. These unmet expectations are sometimes covert, and we may not even be consciously aware of them unless we take time to explore that we are in a negative space. Once we recognize that, we can dive into how we got there and build new practices to help us move back toward a positive space.

Some people find it easy to move back to a positive space, while others seem to gravitate toward a negative space. This may result from upbringing, genetics, and other factors. Regardless of our natural bent or learned tendencies, we *can* move back to a positive space. One great exercise we can do from either a positive or a negative space is to remember positive encounters.

Remember how you filled in the blank at the start? I used to be _____. Take some time to reflect on what you loved about what used to be. (Revisit this exercise in chapter 2 and build from there if you'd like.) At first, this can feel cruel, maybe even like the exact opposite of everything you've tried to do. Why are we trying to make you think of the good that you now lack? Trust us. There is a purpose. Let's say you filled in the blank by saying I used to be <u>married</u>. Maybe you would list that you loved having a companion, the butterfly feeling you'd get when they caressed your face, and the financial security that came from having two incomes.

> Sometimes we slowly move into a negative space, and other times, we experience an automatic switch, feeling catapulted into a negative space.

Now let's unpack each of these. As you remember the good, you can also identify potential areas of unmet needs. If you enjoyed having a companion, it's possible you now feel insecure attending events by yourself. This unmet need may tempt you to isolate rather than attend activities that you'd normally feel excited about. This unusual feeling may leave you empty. But identifying the unmet need exposes some of the root psychological needs that are present. These can be met in other ways—healthy or destructive—as well. You may feel vulnerable, leading you to jump into another relationship just to have a companion. But is this the only option? No way. One alternative to meet the need could be to invite a friend or loved one to attend a concert or other activity with you, giving you a sense of connection to others.

The second need was loving the butterfly feeling that came from the physical touch you received from your spouse. This one is tougher to meet through friends and family, but it's not impossible. What else creates a butterfly feeling? Maybe it's a new adventure, such as mountain biking, taking a cooking class, or visiting a theme park. An adventure with a friend could partially meet a need for excitement that was previously fulfilled by a significant other. As you acknowledge your unmet needs, consider setting up guardrails, reminding yourself that it could be tempting to enter an unhealthy relationship too quickly. Remind yourself that you won't die if you have some unmet needs for a while. If the relationship meets only some physical needs, additional ones may pop up down the road. Again, understanding our needs is important so we know our vulnerabilities. As we build awareness regarding our vulnerabilities, needs, and desires, we can better guard our hearts. Proverbs 4:23 says, "Guard your heart above all else, for it determines the course of your life."

The third need that was met by being married was financial security. Just mentioning money can move many of us into a negative space, but let's explore how recalling the good can help. It could be easy to look at every encounter where you feel pressured to save money and build another brick of resentment. But as you remember the good that used to be, you can recognize that you now have an unmet need. Again, this can be met in numerous ways. Here are just a few of the many options: you could quickly jump into a relationship to gain financial security (please don't choose this option!), tighten up your budget, collaborate with friends about ways to save money, or get a roommate (this one should be carefully calculated as well).

As you remember the good, reflect on the unmet needs you've experienced and how you've met them in positive and negative ways. Look back to chapter 3 for more on positive and negative coping mechanisms. Bring your needs before the Lord and seek His insight as you move forward, trying to meet your needs in healthier ways.

Remembering the Past

Larry was diagnosed with cancer. I, Chuck, remember Larry's investment in my life; he was a mentor and an influential leader. I hurt when I remember Larry's death, so it could be easy to try to avoid thinking about him. I want to hold on to the good memories. Today, as I was writing in my office, I could see a Bible that Larry gave me with a note telling me I did a good job preaching. We don't want to forget the good things simply to avoid feeling hurt. In fact, if we try to avoid thinking about our pain, we'll likely still be triggered to think about the topic when we aren't ready for it. By doing hard work now, we stabilize ourselves mentally so we can be present in our other relationships.

Sometimes we want to avoid thinking about good things from the past to avoid pain. Other times we may avoid thinking about any negative attributes of a person once they pass away. It's almost as if individuals receive a halo after they die. At funeral services, people often speak as if everyone goes to heaven. Why would people do this?

- It feels uncouth to speak poorly of the deceased who is not present to defend themselves.
- It's easier to cope with the loss if people believe their loved one is in a better place.
- They may want to live life as they wish and still believe they, too, will go to heaven someday.

- If people really believe not everyone goes to heaven, they may experience an urgency to speak boldly about God, and that feels scary.

Do you see how complicated our minds can be? To protect ourselves, we may deny what's true. Instead, it's important that we bring God into our grieving process so He can heal our broken minds. Remember, God's armor can protect us better than our own defense mechanisms (Eph. 6:10–17).

What If No Good Came from My Loss?

Are you having a tough time thinking of what you loved? Maybe it's difficult to think of anything good that came from your loss. Remembering positive experiences certainly doesn't mean the loss was worth it. But looking for good offers hope. Sometimes when we get into a negative space, we see only bad things in our lives.

I hurt when I think about the pain I caused Ashley by looking at porn. I also feel disappointed that I dishonored my call to be a man of integrity by lying about it. To avoid feeling slapped in the face with shame all over again if the topic comes up, it could be tempting to get angry. Not much good came from the situation, and if I could go back and behave differently, I would. One good thing that has come from this tragedy is that God has used me to offer accountability and a path to freedom for many men and women. I pray that my vulnerability in discussing my mistakes will help others find hope.

If I knew then what I know now, I could have seen more clearly how greatly it would cost me. We're thankful for how the truth has made our relationship stronger. We cling to God, knowing that His ways truly are so much better than following our own interests.

Looking to God's Word

Let's consider how James encourages us to think:

> Dear brothers and sisters, when troubles of any kind come your way, consider it an opportunity for great joy. For you know that when your faith is tested, your endurance has a chance to grow. So let it grow, for when your endurance is fully developed, you will be perfect and complete, needing nothing. (James 1:2–4)

Yikes. Anyone feeling convicted? We are. Joy isn't the first emotion that comes to mind when we face troubles. But do you remember another verse that says to be transformed by renewing your mind (Rom. 12:2)? Our goal for this chapter is to help you practically work toward transforming your mind. As you look to God for help, asking Him to reveal good things to you, it will create an opportunity for joy. We can use Scripture to help us shift from a negative to a positive space.

We don't *want* the hard times (that would probably be masochistic), but we want to grow stronger. We want to endure. We can be grateful for the growth we experience even if we do not want the trial. Did you run to God during your tough times? If so, be thankful. You became stronger because you ran to Him. Even if you yelled, cussed, or sinned in other ways, run to God. On this earth, we won't reach perfection, but God's perfect love dwells within us and will help us as we call on Him. In fact, Ephesians 2:22 says we are *becoming* a dwelling place for God. This is a process of daily transformation.

> We can use Scripture to help us shift from a negative to a positive space.

We become stronger when we reframe our grief. One way to reframe is to practice a thought-stopping exercise; when a negative experience enters our minds, we stop it. We take the thoughts captive, making them obedient to Christ (2 Cor. 10:5). We focus our eyes on the good things, knowing that we can build joy and endurance.

Let's walk through an example. Imagine you're lonely and you become jealous of a family member who's in a new relationship. First, be aware of why you feel jealous; you're jealous because they have something you value. Perhaps you value connection. God made us for community, so it's good that you value relationship. Second, determine that you don't want to live a jealous life. Recall reasons to be thankful for the family member and for yourself. Choose a replacement thought that you hope to use to help you reframe. For example, you may think, *I want to be happy for them so they can be happy for me later. I'm choosing to be grateful for the opportunities that singleness has brought me, even though I would not have chosen it for myself.* Then you'll be ready to stop the thought when it enters your consciousness again and replay the replacement thought that will guide you to reframe how you feel.

Evaluate how you can reframe your loss to see the strength you need for your next step in life. If you have the courage to talk about your struggles, you can help many others. Invite God to use this situation for His glory.

What Does Grief Produce in Your Life?

Often when we reflect on our losses, we can see ugly parts of our lives that we would rather forget. We may feel out of control, lonely, and unseen. But grief can be a seed that produces more grief, or it can produce gratitude.

Grief can beget more grief—like when Ashley exploded on her family while they were on a boat ride. But it can also beget gratitude. Recently, we were able to get back out on a boat. Because boating had triggered difficult memories, we prepared for the event by praying together and developing an exit strategy. Once we boarded, we were grateful we stayed present with others and thought very little about the past. Consider ways you can coach yourself when you are exposed to memories of your past. Remember, grief can beget gratitude.

Scripture Can Help Us Be Grateful

One verse that ministered to us during our repeated losses was Psalm 30:11, which says,

> You have turned my mourning into joyful dancing.
> You have taken away my clothes of mourning and
> clothed me with joy.

For quite a while, we prayed this verse daily. We printed it out and posted it in our shower so we could direct our thoughts toward God each morning. We prayed, "God, turn our mourning into dancing. We believe You can!" One day, I, Ashley, began to think about this prayer. *How can God change my mourning into dancing?* I contemplated. *One way is to revive my baby who has passed away.* (I prayed this prayer several times with a little one in my womb who had already passed.) Another way was for God to give us the wisdom about whether to journey down the road again. Yet another was for Him to protect the next child. And finally, it came to mind that God could give us the ability to dance, smile, or feel joyful without changing our *circumstances*. After all, one of the fruits of the Spirit is joy. God can do supernaturally what the human mind cannot do on its own. He can do this for you as well. Invite God's Holy Spirit to fill you with joy.

Fill Us with Gratitude, Oh Lord!

Recently, as I rocked our miracle boy, who gladly allowed me to wrap him in a blanket and hold him close, I etched the moment into my mind to the best of my ability. I remember what could have happened. And I hold him close because of it.

This encounter led both of us to see greatness in grief. Wow. That's painful to write. Greatness in grief? Honestly, we don't want any more grief in our lives. We believe we would be most satisfied if we never lost another loved one, hurt anyone with our words, or had to say goodbye to a loved one who moved away. But think about it with us. Grief over our previous losses caused us to hold on to our infant just a little bit longer. It prodded us to thank God for him daily. It caused us to regularly whisper to each other, "He made it!" Grief produced gratitude. But it doesn't naturally do this. It takes God's Holy Spirit. And even then, we're fighting against our flesh!

God,

I want to be able to remember the good things in life, even amid my loss. Help me recognize what blocks my ability to see the good so I can continue to heal. Thank You for the hope I have in You.

Amen.

21 reframing my relationships

MANY OF OUR RELATIONSHIPS are a little broken. Perhaps you wish some people would initiate more or others would leave you alone. If our relationships need work, we can reframe them. How do we do this? First, let's explore some relationship dynamics.

When you think about your closest friends and family members, are the relationships mutually beneficial?[1] Most of us gravitate toward relationships in which we feel both valued and valuable. Look back at the list you created comprised of your support system in chapter 15 on page 125. Who supports whom? Consider creative ways to assess the amount of support each of you invests in the relationship.

For me, Chuck is a large part of my support system. We both agree that we tend to support each other well, so if we use a ratio to describe the value received to value given, we'd say the ratio is about 50:50. But there are days when we give more than we receive. And this is an important part of being in relationship with others.

A while back, I was so ill with a stomach bug that I slept on the floor in the closet next to the bathroom. In the middle of the night, and the next day, I gave very little to the relationship. The ratio quickly moved from 50:50 to 98:2. (I gave myself a 2 because I expressed appreciation to Chuck and the kids for how they took care of me!) Chuck cared for me and the kids, receiving little in return.

Now take a moment to think about how grief impacts your relationships. If we feel weak and needy, the ratios are going to be off. We may be used to feeling like we provide more value than we receive in the relationship. It may be tempting to isolate because we dislike how grief makes us feel vulnerable and needy. But the truth is, we need one another. And it's not all bad to need others. Don't you *need* to feel needed? So do others. Give yourself permission to reach out to someone in your support system and ask them to listen. Make a mental note to return the investment once you feel a little stronger. Their support will help you get back to a place where you can support them. It's also possible that your weakness may increase their sense of value in the relationship.

Have you ever played on a teeter-totter? Accepting support from our loved ones is like playing on a teeter-totter with them. Our support system can give us a push and keep the teeter-totter going. Though we may feel safest when we're both sitting at 50:50, trust is built when the teeter-totter is moving. Additionally, we may experience laughter and a bit of fear, but the mystery of adventure keeps us coming back for more. And they're going to need you to give a push here in a little while, so accept the push they're offering now. They want to play. Soon you'll be able to get back to pulling (or pushing) your own weight.

> Accepting support from our loved ones is like playing on a teeter-totter with them.

Connect with Others Who Have Walked a Similar Path and Have a Positive Outlook

Have you connected with anyone who has faced a similar journey? There is someone out there who has faced loss and still found hope through Christ. Take time to consider your support system. If you don't know someone who has walked a similar road, look online for a blog, a Facebook group, or another online resource to connect you to an overcomer. Join a support group or ask people in your support system if they know of anyone who they'd connect you to.

Consider Jean-Ann's situation. If Jean-Ann had not connected with Cheryl through a grief support ministry, she might still feel stuck. She recalls meeting others who had suffered similar losses and appeared to be doing much better than she felt. This brought both hope and courage. Jean-Ann felt hopeful that if she spent time with these individuals, she could get better. This gave her the courage to speak out, to keep reading and processing, and to continue returning when she felt like hiding. Consider the benefits of inviting someone into your world who has faced a similar path and has had a positive outlook, then commit to being vulnerable with them.

Be Vulnerable

We know it's not easy. We, too, have faced resistance and avoided talking about our losses because it felt like the best way to cope in the moment. But being vulnerable is mutually beneficial in relationships. Sometimes we feel a lot of pressure to be perfect—especially at work, on social media, and for many of us, in our own home. When you're vulnerable and share about your weaknesses, it teaches others that it's all right to be imperfect. This authenticity brings depth to the relationship.

Let's unpack what it means to be vulnerable. When we're vulnerable, we lay down our shields, our masks, whatever it is that protects us and instead invite others to see us as we are. Then, after we have shared, we are impacted by their responses. Sometimes a response is amazing and helpful. Other times it can be overwhelming and painful. It's risky to be vulnerable. Not only is it helpful for us to be vulnerable, but it helps others too. It's mutually beneficial.

Many of us do not want to share because we don't want to hear the response others may offer. Other times we don't want to be vulnerable because doing so will expose a loved one's weakness, and we feel pressure to protect their image. Remember, your willingness to share can be beneficial for others as well. We simply want to prayerfully consider how, when, and with whom to share. We lean toward shining a light on hurt and sin to extinguish its power; however, we want to be careful not to engage in a power struggle or to retaliate. Instead, we challenge you to invite God into your negative spaces to help you reframe the way you see yourself and others.

> God,
>
> You are my Redeemer. You take care of me even when I don't see it. You bring beauty from this sinful world. Thank You for creating me to have amazing relationships. You want things to be good. Help me learn to reframe.
>
> Amen.

22 | a transformative expression

HAVE YOU EVER WONDERED how a cancer research foundation began? Or why so many people are willing to pay to run a 5K early on a cold morning to support a rare disease? Many of the individuals behind these great projects have reframed their loss, choosing to build strength so they could help others rather than simply protecting themselves in their grieving state. People like you and me realize that sometimes thinking of all that we've lost can get the best of us; we would rather focus on what we have and hold on to hope for a better future. This mode of reframing can be transformative.

Have you considered making something big out of your loss? If not, why don't you pause a second and ask God how He might bring beauty from the ashes (Isa. 61:3)? Or have you considered using art to help you process your loss? Even if you don't consider yourself a crafty person, we believe there are some creative tools that can be used to bring healing to your soul. And many of them require very little artistic talent. Before we give a few examples, let's chat about the reasons artistic expression can bring healing.

The hard work of reframing our losses can be taxing. But art can feel fun, bringing levity to a tough time. Art has a way of setting free some emotions that may be difficult to express with words. This project has the power to do several things: build a lasting connection to who or what was lost, help you transition to who you are now, integrate this loss into your life, and help you move forward.

Traditional and Not-So-Traditional Creative Expressions

Some examples of artistic or creative forms of expression include physical creations, events, businesses, or music. You may or may not have the talent to write a song that will be a hit, but your song can bring freedom to your grieving soul. And who knows? It could turn out better than you thought and help others down the road. Be adventurous. Be vulnerable.

> Art has a way of setting free some emotions that may be difficult to express with words.

Inventors spend much of their time working on problems. They examine what needs to be better. They're in the business of fixing what isn't working. People who struggled to choose a major in college have developed career assessments. Individuals who have faced divorce have founded support groups for divorced individuals. Single dads have started social media groups to help other dads who feel alone. Your artistic expression could be painting a portrait, sculpting a piece of pottery, or writing a poem. But it could also be developing a resource, a service, or an activity that will help you or others process loss.

If you lost a loved one due to death, you could include one of the person's physical possessions in the project. You may use a clothing item, one of their favorite books, a coffee mug, a knife, or sewing supplies to help inspire creativity. For example, Rue's father loved coffee. Rue was not a coffee drinker but decided to keep one of his father's favorite mugs. As he considered options for the mug, he decided to take it to work and put his pens in it. That way, he would feel connected to his father throughout the day. See? We weren't tricking you when we said your artistic expression doesn't have to require major art talent. Simply taking a little bit of time and applying some divergent thinking can bring healing and excitement to our lives.

Are you a little more ambitious? Consider completing a therapeutic paint-pouring project, which we explain in a blog post.[1] Maybe you want to go on a trip and celebrate a loved one's life. Chris did just that. He invited his younger brother, Nate, to take a trip to the West Coast. They wanted to honor the life of their older brother, Colin, who had died by suicide a few years earlier. As young kids, the three boys dreamed about taking a trip to the West Coast. One night, after Chris grew angry when someone mentioned going on vacation, he realized he was upset because he felt he would never be able to take the trip they had dreamed about. Angry with Colin, angry with life, he sat. After a few moments, he decided that Colin would want him to take the trip.

When Chris and Nate planned the trip, they decided to include some of Colin's favorite things to help them feel close to him. They developed a playlist of Colin's favorite songs, ate some of his favorite foods, and visited the landmarks they had dreamed about as kids. Together, Chris and Nate laughed, cried, and made memories. The trip wasn't what they'd dreamt it would be. But reality rarely turns out to be just like a dream, and the experience brought healing nonetheless. Would planning a trip help you heal?

If you've lost a loved one due to divorce, you may sarcastically remark, "Yep. This one's for me. I'm going on a trip to do *all* the things I was not able to do while I was married." Please don't take that trip. And if it's already scheduled, reframe it. Please enjoy your freedom, but devoting an entire trip to celebrating hurt can actually create more grief. So be sure your artistic expression is developed while you're in a positive space; this enables you to neutralize some triggers and build a life in a positive space.

If you lost a loved one to death, imagine what would make them happy if they were still around. If the person loved Christmas, decorate. If they were an educator, become a tutor or start a scholarship. Ven needed to sell his father's house, and he wanted to have something special from the home. The property had trees, so he cut one down and built a table. Be creative and use your unique talents. How can you create an opportunity to heal through your artistic expression?

Remember to love. Cherish life.

Artistic Expression in the Bible

In Joshua 3, God had just allowed the Israelites to cross the Jordan River. God used Joshua to part the river, instructing him to tell the leaders and priests to carry the ark of the covenant *into* the water. The instructions were specific. Once in the water, they were expected to wait. They may have felt a little more secure standing on the shore. Waiting can be difficult; but as they waited, they began to see and *feel* God's hand move. Imagine how their feet felt as the sand shifted underneath them. The river stood up like a wall, and they were able to pass on dry land. In Joshua 4, God instructed Joshua to choose twelve men, each of whom would select a stone to carry out of the river to build a memorial that would serve as a reminder about what God had done. As you read the passage, consider why God wanted them to build a memorial.

It was there at Gilgal that Joshua piled up the twelve stones taken from the Jordan River.

Then Joshua said to the Israelites, "In the future your children will ask, 'What do these stones mean?' Then you can tell them, 'This is where the Israelites crossed the Jordan on dry ground.' For the LORD your God dried up the river right before your eyes, and he kept it dry until you were all across, just as he did at the Red Sea when he dried it up until we had all crossed over. He did this so all the nations of the earth might know that the LORD's hand is powerful, and so you might fear the LORD your God forever." (Josh. 4:20–24)

God wants us to remember the ways He takes care of us. Can you identify some ways God has cared for you through your loss? Perhaps you're living in the moment when sand is sliding out from under your feet; hold fast, God's hand may be working.

Contemplate how God is leading you. Let's say you decide to make a piece of art. In the future, people may ask, "What does this piece of art mean?" We pray you can tell them how the Lord has healed your soul, day by day. In addition to serving others, these special pieces are reminders to us as well. When you're drifting into a negative space, may your artistic expression remind you of your reliance on God, His healing power, and your ability to endure.

God,

Help me reframe my loss using something I can hold or see. May this work serve as a memorial of Your transformative power [Josh. 4:4–7].

Amen.

23 | reframing my title

THIS IS NO LONGER OUR BOOK. It is your book. Take another look at the title—*I Used to Be* _____. How did you fill in the blank?

Process your growth and any small steps you've made toward healing. Has your soul experienced a transformation? If so, let's think about that phrase again. Would it be possible to fill in the blank differently in the future? For example, let's say you filled in the blank as "I used to be <u>married</u>." How would you fill in the blank now that you've grown a bit? Could you say, "I used to be <u>broken</u>" or "I used to be <u>stuck</u>"?

After our second loss, I, Chuck, was aware that I couldn't protect my children. I used to be <u>a protector</u>. Also, I used to be <u>hiding</u>. Now I find freedom in being honest with myself and others, remembering that I don't have to pretend to have it all together. Before facing loss, I, Ashley, felt like I used to be <u>strong</u>. After years of processing and learning how to handle triggers, emotions, and fears, we can say, "We used to be <u>deficient</u>." We can look back and see growth or hurt.

Take time to look back and see growth. It isn't completely true that we were perfectly strong or totally deficient. But the way we see our world greatly impacts our beliefs about

176 | reframing grief

ourselves. We can learn to recognize that we may be in a negative space when our beliefs feel unsteady. It's time to train ourselves to recognize that we may need some nutrition, sleep, or
time with God to help us move back to
a positive mental space. The truth is,
we probably aren't as bad as we think.
On our best days, neither are we as
good as we think we are. Keeping this
in mind helps us stay grounded.

> It's time to train ourselves to recognize that we may need some nutrition, sleep, or time with God to help us move back to a positive mental space.

Consider Willum's story. He experienced years of mistreatment by his
dad, then lost him suddenly. This
threatened Willum's stability. Perhaps
if he had picked up this book at the beginning of his journey, he would have
whispered to himself, "I used to be
stable." But as Willum turned to God for healing, he was able
to identify his unmet needs, practice healthy coping mechanisms, and reclaim what was lost; he came out victorious. Now
he can fill in the blank and declare, "I used to be unstable."

Now it's your turn. How would you reframe your title? Don't
rush this exercise. Sit. Walk. Pray. Ask God to search your heart
and show you areas where growth has occurred. Next month,
when you see this book on a shelf, what will encourage you? If
you face another loss, how might you feel again in the future?
What will remind your future hurting self that you are resilient and you can get through this suffering? In fact, consider
if you still feel the same level of pain as when you read the title
for the first time. If not, it's possible that you've grown! You
likely picked up this book because you felt like you used to be
stronger. Have your efforts brought strength?

For extra credit, grab a pencil (or a marker if you dare) and
fill in the blank on the front cover of your book. We want you

to see this book as a symbol of your ability to overcome, to reframe your loss. Rather than remembering that you used to be strong and no longer are, what if you looked at your weakness and accepted that you grieved, which is normal and causes people to feel a bit weak, but you rose in triumph? Seriously. Go get a marker and write on this book. Be sure to write on the spine as well since that's likely the part you'll see if you place it on a bookshelf.

You've done so much work building strength. In what ways have you grown stronger? You have looked at your positive and negative coping mechanisms and opted to address your personal needs in a positive way. You have examined the pain caused by your loss and determined to reengage rather than withdraw. You have reached out to positive forces, family, and friends and asked for what you needed. You have shown courage and built resilience. You are not the same. You have repaired your broken frame and *should* see yourself differently.

Tell yourself, "I used to be _____."

God,

You, not my losses, define me. Help me continue to reframe the way I look at myself so I can move forward, finding meaning and helping others.

Amen.

moving forward

Wow. We're nearing the end of our journey together. We've done some tough work. We've looked at the unseen elements of grief as they relate to ourselves, our world, and our loved ones. We've reframed our grief. Where do we go from here? As we take a few steps, sometimes we will be impressed with how strong we seem to appear; other times we may feel crushed by defeat, wondering why we're still struggling so deeply. That's okay and is normal.

Think about what you can offer others. Perhaps it's as simple as letting them know that it's normal to ebb and flow, to cry, to be strong, to be needy, to lack answers, to *just* be. But in the process, let's determine to keep inviting God into our negative spaces.

24 where to go from here

KUDOS TO YOU! You have spent time healing. Hopefully you feel ready to think about the future. Don't worry. We aren't going to encourage you to leave the past behind and forget about your grief. We believe doing so would be impossible, but we've found that looking toward a hopeful future gives us the ability to "release" a little bit of our hurt as we proceed into the great unknown. Hopefully the work you've done has neutralized some triggers. For example, many days we drive by the hospital and don't think of the loss of our babies anymore. Sometimes we pray for the ambulance drivers who speed past. Other times we're casually talking with the boys and aren't triggered. One of our goals is to find ways to trigger loving memories rather than pain and suffering.

Forward Movement

Humans prefer forward motion. We don't like falling behind and tend to get discouraged if we lack forward momentum. When we don't like the way the future looks, we backpedal, resist, and maybe even beg God to make it stop. This can happen with any loss. Although we want to move forward, the process is different for each individual and each loss, possibly requiring different steps for you than for others.

We've moved forward by building community, hustling, and rebuilding trust. When I faced miscarriage, I prayed, researched medical options, read academic journal articles, and connected with the kids. When my dad was diagnosed with cancer, we spent extra time together. I walked with him as he recovered, called him more frequently, and cherished our time together. We've laid down our pride by asking for what we need. And you know what? It has gotten easier for us. Perhaps it will get easier for you if you determine to keep moving forward, inviting God into the process. And today, we still have seasons where fear creeps in. Our losses changed us. We moved forward by establishing accountability and working to communicate and connect with each other spiritually.

How Will I Move Forward?

If you're ready to join a support group, do it. If you need time but think a support group could be useful in the future, think about a specific time when you hope to try to reach out for community. Where will you go? Explore why you don't yet feel ready and set goals to help you become ready to receive support down the road. If a support group isn't for you, what options are you considering?

Forward movement, even at a slow pace, will help you maintain and build courage that will help you in the future.

Whether you meet with a pastor, counselor, coach, friend, or family member, determine to keep moving. Commit to spending time daily in God's Word. The Bible corrects, guides, and trains us (2 Tim. 3:16–17). Forward movement, even at a slow pace, will help you maintain and build courage that will help you in the future.

What Should I Expect as I Try to Move Forward?

Sometimes our unrealistic expectations set us up to feel bad about ourselves. These expectations can come from others as well. Someone may say, "It will get better." And when things feel worse, we blame ourselves or feel broken.

After we lost our second child, we felt worse on day two than on day one. This was overwhelming and we grew concerned about the possibility of intensifying pain in the subsequent days. During all our losses, we felt a little less mentally stable than usual. As we moved forward, it was important to engage in self-care, especially getting rest and connecting with one another spiritually. But sleep felt more difficult, and connecting spiritually meant allowing each other in when being guarded felt safer. Although it was important to care for ourselves, it wasn't easy.

Grief and Joy Can Occur at Once

Anytime we face change, it's normal to encounter strong emotions. If you find it difficult to experience emotions such as joy or excitement, or you feel guilty for smiling, ask yourself, "Who's in charge of me?" If you experience guilt, who's speaking guilt into your life? Be curious about why you feel what you feel. Emotions alert us that a behavior or experience is happening. It's up to you to decide how you will think and behave in response to the alerts. If you are alerted to both grief and joy simultaneously, you are free to choose how to respond.

When grief and joy occur at the same time, it feels unusual—because it is. You're experiencing cognitive dissonance.[1] Simply put, cognitive dissonance is the collision of two conflicting thoughts or emotions. Our minds try to reconcile which thought or idea is true or acceptable. For example, if we're happy and sad at the same time, the discomfort we feel is cognitive dissonance. It's okay to feel both happy and sad, so if you accept the experience as normal, you should be able to reconcile the dissonance. We're resilient and can learn how to think deeply and sit with our feelings for a little while. If you lost a loved one to death and they were able to see you, would it bring them peace and joy to see you miserable? They'd probably be saddened to see you hurting. They loved you and wanted to bring life to your soul. Loving again seems like betrayal, but feel them release you to love!

Emotions alert us that a behavior or experience is happening.

How many hours have you spent sitting with your grief? Hopefully fewer than ten thousand hours. In the book *Outliers*, Malcolm Gladwell writes that after about ten thousand hours of an activity, we begin to demonstrate exceptional skill.[2] It's okay if we're amateurs and don't have ten thousand hours of grief experience logged, but we can get better at allowing emotions to be present without letting them overpower our lives. You can worship during your suffering. You can become angry and hold your tongue. You can experience a trigger while at work and push through. You can cry when you would rather hold it together. You can laugh and cry at the same time. You can sob. And then you can get up, wash your face, and go about your day. This is normal.

We are complex people, and on this earth, we may never be as fully seen as we desire. And sometimes we will be seen much more than we wish. We will feel exposed and want to hide. This is what it means to be human, to love, and to lose what we love.

> God,
>   I'm ready to move forward, even if it's just a little bit at a time. Show me where to go from here. Help me reach out to people who will journey with me as I take a step forward. Thank You for Your support.
>
> > Amen.

25 processing what I have learned

CONSIDER THE LESSONS grief has taught you. One thing we came to understand is that we really don't comprehend what people are carrying. When we walk into a room with hundreds of people, hundreds of movies are playing. We have entered a scene in their movie, but we don't know the plot or the conflict they've faced. And sometimes we're so focused on our own movie that we don't even take time to consider other plot twists in the movies going on around us.

When we have lost loved ones to death, we've remembered how important it is to keep focused on eternity because life on earth is temporary. We've also learned to hold on to our loved ones a bit more tightly. And we've seen God use our pain to teach us lessons that we can teach others. When we watched bosses, ministry leaders, and friends have affairs, we noticed that there seems to be a mental process people follow before they cheat. We prayed about this process and drafted illustrations to identify what might be going on internally so we could work backward. In time, we helped others intervene before it was too late. A portion of this process led to the development of Switch Theory.

What have you learned through your losses?

If people have told you how to feel and how not to feel, you probably won't do that to others.

If you stood at a loved one's funeral and felt weighed down by other people's grief stories, you may intend to be a better listener at the next funeral you attend.

If, on the day of your greatest loss, you were driving and were hurt by someone who honked at you when you sat at a red light a little longer than they wanted you to, you may be more patient while driving.

What other ways has your hurt helped you empathize with others, care for neighbors, or make investments in your personal self-care? We've learned that reaching out, even when done imperfectly, is the right thing to do. We've also learned to trust that our emotions may indicate something is awry. When we've tuned in to our emotions and invited God into the situation, we've prevented ourselves from engaging in negative behavior.

Grief can reveal what's beneath the surface that's been ignored or unseen. Grief makes you more of what you already are. Grief can expose distant relationships, inner strength, a weak relationship with God, an experience of anonymity at work that feels unbearable, and so many other opportunities for relational growth. You are resilient. If you feel like your relationships are lacking, you can do something about it. If that's your situation, sit for a moment and think of ways to strengthen the relationships around you.

> What other ways has your hurt helped you empathize with others, care for neighbors, or make investments in your personal self-care?

Have you struggled with your relationship with God because of your losses? Or have you experienced a closeness unlike any other? Through some of our losses, we felt closer to God than ever, while at other times, we experienced such distance that it broke our hearts. But we learned to lean on God's Word in a new way. Our emotions told us that God felt more distant than usual, so as we read Scripture, we were drawn to the stories of Job (Job 6:24; 30:20; 34:29), David (Ps. 13:1–3; 22:1–3), Isaiah (Isa. 42:14; 64:7), Abraham (Gen. 12:2; 16:15–17; 17:17–18; 21:1–2), Jonah (Jonah 2:4), and Jesus (Matt. 27:46), who faced periods of silence or distance from God. And all these men were led on a journey to places that were emotionally and physically exhausting. And God

> Grief can expose distant relationships, inner strength, a weak relationship with God, an experience of anonymity at work that feels unbearable, and so many other opportunities for relational growth.

was worthy of their service, worthy of their suffering. We knew this. This helped us focus on the fact that God is still worthy of our praise even if He doesn't bless us with immediately answered prayers. We have learned to trust even when it's tough. We anticipate that we will need to read these words again in the future. Grief lessons. They aren't easy, but God's Word tells us, "Blessed are those who mourn" (Matt. 5:4 NIV).

Have you read the book of Ecclesiastes? Many find this book depressing. We recently concluded a teaching series about it, and some people thought it was odd we were teaching on the subject. But there were some powerful moments. The main takeaway from the book is this: Solomon had more wisdom, riches, and power than anyone before him. He experienced amazing food, educational insights, and sexual pleasures, yet he didn't find true meaning in these things. He determined that, apart from God, everything is meaningless. But with God, we find purpose that is unattainable by any other means. How comforting!

Because we live in a world with endless advertisements enticing us to pursue pleasures at the click of a button, it's reassuring to remember that God is our true source of meaning. If we find our worth in Christ, we will be okay. This understanding provides roots that will hold us in the next storm as well (Matt. 7:25; Eph. 3:17–19).

God,

Thank You that I can learn new ways to think, finding meaning in You. Deepen my roots so that no storm can pull me away from You.

Amen.

26 I have something to offer others

AS YOU'VE THOUGHT about what you have learned, have you also considered ways you can help others? You may have caught your breath and feel ready to pass on the oxygen mask. If not, take a few more breaths, go back to chapter 1, and process your grief a bit more. Get a coach, find a friend. Keep moving. And when you get back to this chapter, you'll find that passing the oxygen helps you pay it forward and make the world a better place. Actually, it may also help you process your grief in deeper ways like it did for our friend Alex. He lost his wife to cancer. A few months after her death, he was talking to someone who had just lost their spouse to the same type of cancer. Alex not only found encouragement from the conversation with someone who was walking a journey like his, but he was also able to pour out support to someone in need of connection. God made us for relationship. In 2 Corinthians 1:4, we are encouraged, "He comforts us in all our troubles so that we can comfort others. When they are troubled, we will be able to give them the same comfort God has given us."

When we withdraw from relationship, we find ourselves hurting. When we commit to healing and connection, we find deeper levels of purpose. Psalm 84:6 says, "When they walk through the Valley of Weeping, it will become a place of refreshing springs." The Valley of Weeping is also known as the Valley of Baca or a desert place.[1] Can you visualize that imagery for a moment? You are walking through the desert and turn around to see that each place you've stepped has become a luscious body of water, teeming with life.

How do we ensure that we're able to help others? We must be aware of what's in our heart, taking it before the Lord and asking Him to expose our thoughts and behaviors that create distance between us and Him (Ps. 139:23–24). Luke 6:45 tells us that "the mouth speaks what the heart is full of" (NIV). So when our mouth spills out doubt, hurtful words, or endless grief, let's run to God. His Spirit will fill us if we ask. Consider how good is stored up in our hearts. We meditate on the Lord (Ps. 1:2). We take our negative thoughts to God, asking for His insight. He will help us take our thoughts captive, remembering that God is our Lord, not our thoughts (2 Cor. 10:5). And we guard our hearts (Prov. 4:23) by thinking about things that are honorable to God (Phil. 4:8). As we learn to lean on Christ, allowing Him to fill us, we can be poured out to help others. As you've seen throughout this book, we will still fall short. But when we run to God, He makes us better. He makes us more like Him.

> God made us for relationship. When we withdraw from relationship, we find ourselves hurting.

You're needed. Someone else needs oxygen. Someone else needs to be seen.

Practical Ways I Can Help Others

In addition to the creative and artistic expressions discussed in chapter 22, there are thousands of ways you can help others who are grieving. Before we share a few ideas, we encourage you to take a moment and ask God to bring to mind someone who has lost something or someone. Do you have time, talent, or treasures you could share with that person? Invite God to help you think of ways you could encourage them. It's amazing how God will anoint our willingness to ask Him this question. And when we support those who are in need, it brings glory to our Savior (Matt. 25:34–40).

Below is a list of some practical ways you can encourage someone who is grieving.

- Attend a grief support group, workshop, or conference (online or in person) with someone who is grieving. (We recommend using RightNow Media if you have access.[2] The site is designed to be used by individuals, churches, small groups, and organizations.)
- Write a card or create a video message to send the person, letting them know you're thinking of them. Pray for them. (You get bonus points for actually praying for them rather than simply saying you will pray for them.)
- Invite the person to complete a reading plan on the YouVersion Bible App with you. Search for our plans to complete together![3]
- Pick them up and take them out for coffee or whatever mutual activity you enjoy.
- If the person has children, offer to babysit or pay a babysitter for them so they can engage in self-care. Find others to donate time or money and purchase a massage or restaurant gift card.
- Create and share a playlist of songs that have encouraged you throughout your journey.
- Write the person's name on a sticky note and place it in your shower or on your bathroom mirror or another

visible place at home or work. Pray for the person daily. Occasionally, send them a reminder that you're thinking of them, including a Bible verse that resonated with you during your loss.

- Start a meal train.
- Send the person a link to a podcast, book, or other resource you've found useful.

If you're still amid your grief and feel one of these tools could be helpful for you, try asking a loved one to support you in one of the ways listed above.

Pushing Past Fear

It can be quite scary to reach out to someone who is hurting, but oftentimes the most valuable things in life bring a little fear. When I, Ashley, was in college, one of my professors shared that he and his family had lost a second child due to being stillborn. As I wrote him a card, I cried. I threw the card across the room, knowing that my words weren't enough. I wanted to rip it up. I almost did. But I went ahead and stuck the card in the envelope and sealed it, determined to give it to him. Several months later, while in a different course with the professor, in front of the class, he mentioned my card and how meaningful it was. Now, it's been almost fifteen years, and the experience still surfaces from time to time.

It's easy to dismiss an idea to reach out to someone, but we've seen how valuable it can be. Why did I feel compelled to write a card to my professor? I hadn't experienced my own pregnancy loss at that time. But I had lost four siblings due to miscarriage. I had suffered. I had grieved. Though I wasn't in his shoes, when he shared, my grief was triggered. In this situation, grief begat empathy. I remembered the love I had for those babies and how heartbreaking it was to lose them, even as a small child. I acknowledged that he and his family had to be suffering greatly, so I did what a poor college student could do. I prayed and wrote a card. And no, it wasn't enough. Nothing we can do is ever enough to take away the pain of grief. But our actions show the receiver that we see them, and sometimes God uses our kindness to show others that He sees them too.

> Our actions show the receiver that we see them, and sometimes God uses our kindness to show others that He sees them too.

With practice, we can become more comfortable providing support to others. For example, we can pray for people before surgery and visit them in the hospital. If you have a skill, ask God to help you use it. If you have financial resources, be generous. If you have time but limited resources, you may be able to make the biggest impact of all. Grieving people need connection, especially to Jesus. And Jesus stood in our place and is now allowing us to stand in His place, representing Him to those who are hurting. We are the light of the world (Matt. 5:14).

God,
    I want to heal, and I acknowledge that part of that healing can come through helping others. Help me see how my story can encourage and comfort someone else in their loss. Please send me out to those who have a need.
                                        Amen.

27 becoming the best version of me

IN CHAPTER 23, we introduced the idea of reframing the title of this book. Have you done so? Rather than seeing yourself as weak (I used to be <u>strong</u>), have you been able to see some of your strengths?

This side of heaven, none of us will "arrive" at a place where we are completely whole. We are going to remain works in progress. We press on toward the goal for the prize (Phil. 3:14).

As you press on, fill in the blanks: I used to be _____. I am _____. I will be _____. Here's an example: I used to be <u>crippled with grief</u>. I am <u>working through my loss, determined to help myself so I can help others</u>. I will be <u>victorious, in Jesus's name</u>!

Becoming My Best

As you commit to the process that God teaches in His Word, you should continue to see measurable progress over time. Below are a few tips to becoming the best version of yourself, even through loss:

- Evaluate how you use your time. Do you feel pleased with the amount of time you spend at work, with family, using technology, or in worship?
- Consider who you're spending your time with and the impact they make on your spiritual growth and healing. Who needs more time? Who needs less time?
- Ask God to help you see who is Lord over your thoughts. If you don't like your thoughts, engage in practices that bring God into the midst of even the darkest ones. We didn't get data on this, but we're pretty sure that no one has eaten a cookie while praying, "Lord, help me resist eating a cookie." We tend to separate ourselves from corrective thoughts when we want to go our own way. Bethany Barnard sings a beautiful song called "God Have Your Way in Me." It says, "There's a way that seems right to me, but it leads to death."[1] This comes from Proverbs 14:12 and 16:25. Lead us, Lord! Correct the thoughts that pull us away from You.
- Contemplate ways to improve your physical health habits by committing to move your body and fueling it with nutritious and delicious foods. Also seek medical attention whenever you're being alerted that something seems off.
- Track your sleep so you understand the ideal number of hours you need to thrive.
- Make time for fun. Commit to laughter and adventure. Stay humble, and sit on the floor and play make-believe with kids in your family, at church, or in your community.
- Assess and manage stress. Your body provides signals when you demand more from it than it is designed to give.

Who Does God Say I Am?

God says you are loved (John 3:16). He sees you (Ps. 139). God says you are able. You can be strong and courageous, resisting fear and discouragement because His presence is enough (Josh. 1:9). You can stay committed to God, even if you lose everything (Job 1:21). You are forgiven, redeemed, and set free (Eph. 1:7; Gal. 5:1). And you are commissioned to go. We declare that you used to be lost. Now you are saved. You will be used by God to bring healing and hope to others. May God use your story.

> We declare that you used to be lost. Now you are saved. You will be used by God to bring healing and hope to others.

How do you fill in the blanks?

I used to be _____. I am _____. I will be _____.

God,

Thank You for transforming me into a new creation. I am still a work in progress, but I acknowledge Your work in my life and in my grief. I choose You. I choose to continue becoming who You called me to be. I am a child of God.

Amen.

acknowledgments

THE VISION FOR THIS BOOK was formed out of our grief. First, we want to acknowledge God as the writer of our story, the One who makes beauty from ashes and enabled us to survive the journey, helped us heal, and empowered us to lead others to Him. Secondly, we want to acknowledge our babies. They lost their lives, and we didn't get to see them thrive. The moments we had with them shaped us, and this book wouldn't have happened without this impact.

Regarding the effort it took to bring this book to the reader, we are so thankful to those who believed in our work. Chip, thanks for hustling throughout the pandemic, seeing the importance of the topic despite the difficult season we were in. Thanks to everyone at Revell who helped with editing, design, and marketing. Thanks to our friends Joe and Adam. Your early editorial recommendations and encouragement helped us improve this work.

Rachel, Amy, Sarah, and Carson, you've given of yourselves to ensure this project is successful, and we're so grateful. We also acknowledge that some of you experienced loss along this journey. We're thankful you chose to lean in instead of leaning out. We've prayed for you and are honored to work together.

We want to thank our parents and sons; you have made sacrifices and supported us on this journey. You have ministered alongside us and played a crucial role in our success. Thanks to Nick, Amanda, and others who have stepped in so we could travel. You have helped keep the rhythm in our home, and for that, we're so thankful.

We appreciate so many people at Bethel Church in Evansville, Indiana, for seeing something in us and providing an opportunity to serve, lead, and speak.

notes

Chapter 6 Giving Myself Permission to Grieve

1. Shane and Shane, "Psalm 13," track 3 on *Psalms*, WellHouse Records, 2002.

2. W. Murray Severance and Terry Eddinger, *That's Easy for You to Say: Your Quick Guide to Pronouncing Bible Names* (Nashville: Broadman & Holman, 1997), 170.

Chapter 7 Exploring Defense Mechanisms

1. Sigmund Freud began conversations about defense mechanisms, and his daughter, Anna Freud, developed them further. See Sigmund Freud, "Inhibitions, Symptoms, and Anxiety," in *Standard Edition of the Complete Psychological Works of Sigmund Freud*, ed. and trans. J. Strachey, vol. 20 (London: Hogarth Press, 1926); Anna Freud, *The Ego and the Mechanisms of Defense* (New York: International Universities Press, 1946).

2. Lee Ross, "The Intuitive Psychologist and His Shortcomings: Distortions in the Attribution Process," in *Advances in Experimental Social Psychology*, ed. L. Berkowitz (New York: Academic Press, 1977), 10.

Chapter 11 How I Look at Changes around Me

1. Alan J. Hawkins, Brian J. Willoughby, and William J. Doherty, "Reasons for Divorce and Openness to Marital Reconciliation," *Journal of Divorce & Remarriage* 53, no. 6 (2012): 453–63, https://doi.org/10.1080/10502556.2012.682898.

Chapter 12 Work-Grief Balance

1. Stephen Moeller, "Grief in the Workplace," The Grief Recovery Method, July 7, 2017, https://www.griefrecoverymethod.com/blog/2017/07/grief-workplace.

2. Bethel Music, "No Longer Slaves," *We Will Not Be Shaken*, Bethel Music, 2015.

Chapter 13 Spiritual Matters

1. John Fisher coined the term *spiritual dissonance*, but we take a slightly different approach with it. John W. Fisher, "Spiritual Health: Its Nature and Place in the School Curriculum" (PhD diss., University of Melbourne, 1998).

Chapter 14 How Grief Impacts My Intimate Relationships

1. Alexandra Killewalde, "Money, Work, and Marital Stability: Assessing Change in the Gendered Determinants of Divorce," *American Sociological Review* 81, no. 4 (2016): 696–719, https://www.asanet.org/sites/default/files/attach/journals/aug16asrfeature.pdf.

2. Katherine Gold, Ananda Sen, and Rodney A. Hayward, "Marriage and Cohabitation Outcomes after Pregnancy Loss," *Pediatrics* 125, no. 5 (2010): 1202–07, https://pubmed.ncbi.nlm.nih.gov/20368319/.

Chapter 15 How Others Respond to My Loss

1. Jennie Allen, *Find Your People: Building Deep Community in a Lonely World* (Colorado Springs: Waterbrook, 2022), 76.

2. For another great resource that will help you explore your anger, check out Creative Therapy's poster: https://www.creativetherapystore.com/products/managing-your-anger-poster.

Chapter 16 My Altered Support System

1. Romesh Diwan, "Relational Wealth and the Quality of Life," *Journal of Socio-Economics* 29 (2000): 305–40, https://www.sciencedirect.com/science/article/abs/pii/S1053535700000731.

2. Visit https://hopemommies.org/hope-boxes.

3. Brittany Rust, "Finding God in Your Miscarriage," YouVersion, accessed October 31, 2022, https://www.bible.com/reading-plans/13213-finding-god-in-your-miscarriage.

Chapter 18 Asking for What I Need

1. Miller McPherson, Lynn Smith-Lovin, and Matthew E. Brashears, "Social Isolation in America: Changes in Core Discussion Networks over Two Decades," *American Sociological Review* 71, no. 3 (2006): 353–75, http://www.jstor.org/stable/30038995.

Chapter 21 Reframing My Relationships

1. For more about challenges that may result from efforts to establish mutually beneficial relationships, check out the following study: Joan Monin et al., "Gender Differences in Short-Term Cardiovascular Effects of Giving and Receiving Support for Health Concerns in Marriage," *Health Psychology* 38, no. 10 (2019): 936–47, https://doi.org/10.1037/hea0000777.

Chapter 22 A Transformative Expression

1. Ashley Elliott, "Love and Loss Project," Chuck and Ashley, September 28, 2022, www.chuckandashley.com/post/love-and-loss-project.

Chapter 24 Where to Go from Here

1. Leon Festinger, *A Theory of Cognitive Dissonance* (Stanford: Stanford University Press, 1957).
2. Malcom Gladwell, *Outliers: The Story of Success* (New York: Little, Brown and Co., 2008), 40.

Chapter 26 I Have Something to Offer Others

1. Charles John Ellicott, ed., *A Bible Commentary for English Readers* (London: Cassell and Co., 1905), at Psalm 84:6.
2. See www.rightnowmedia.com.
3. Find our reading plans on YouVersion and at chuckandashley.com. Some of our plans include "Love and Loss," "When a Couple Loses a Baby: A Man's Perspective," "Child of God," "Praying for My Future Spouse," "Prayer Boot Camp," and "Spiritual Intimacy as Couples."

Chapter 27 Becoming the Best Version of Me

1. Bethany Barnard, "God Have Your Way in Me," track 4 on *A Better Word*, 2017.

Chuck and Ashley Elliott are content creators who have partnered with YouVersion, RightNow Media, and other international organizations to equip people to build spiritual and relational success. Chuck, as a pastor, and Ashley, as a counselor, have devoted their lives to help people fight negativity and leave a legacy. They are advisory board members for the AACC's International Christian Coaching Association (ICCA) and have earned master's degrees in counseling, education, and organizational leadership. Chuck and Ashley live in Indiana with their three sons.

To connect with Chuck and Ashley online, visit ChuckandAshley.com and find them on social media: Facebook @ ChuckandAshley, Instagram @ChuckandAshleyCoaching, Twitter @AshleyChuckAnd, and YouTube @ChuckAshley.